Extreme Programming Installed

Installed

The XP Series

Kent Beck, Series Advisor

Extreme Programming, familiarly known as XP, is a discipline of the business of software development that focuses the whole team on common, reachable goals. Using the values and principles of XP, teams apply appropriate XP practices in their own context. XP practices are chosen for their encouragement of human creativity and their acceptance of human frailty. XP teams produce quality software at a sustainable pace.

One of the goals of XP is to bring accountability and transparency to software development, to run software development like any other business activity. Another goal is to achieve outstanding results—more effective and efficient development with far fewer defects than is currently expected. Finally, XP aims to achieve these goals by celebrating and serving the human needs of everyone touched by software development—sponsors, managers, testers, users, and programmers.

The XP series exists to explore the myriad variations in applying XP. While XP began as a methodology addressing small teams working on internal projects, teams worldwide have used XP for shrink-wrap, embedded, and large-scale projects as well. The books in the series describe how XP applies in these and other situations, addressing both technical and social concerns.

Change has come to software development. However, change can be seen as an opportunity, not a threat. With a plan for change, teams can harness this opportunity to their benefit. XP is one such plan for change.

Titles in the Series

Extreme Programming Applied: Playing to Win, Ken Auer and Roy Miller

Extreme Programming Explained, Second Edition: Embrace Change, Kent Beck with Cynthia Andres

Extreme Programming Explored, William C. Wake

Extreme Programming for Web Projects, Doug Wallace, Isobel Raggett, and Joel Aufgang

Extreme Programming Installed, Ron Jeffries, Ann Anderson, and Chet Hendrickson

Planning Extreme Programming, Kent Beck and Martin Fowler

Testing Extreme Programming, Lisa Crispin and Tip House

Extreme Programming
Installed

Ron Jeffries
Ann Anderson
Chet Hendrickson

ADDISON-WESLEY

Boston • San Francisco • New York • Toronto • Montreal
London • Munich • Paris • Madrid
Capetown • Sydney • Tokyo • Singapore • Mexico City

Many of the designations used by manufacturers and sellers to distinguish their products are claimed as trademarks. Where those designations appear in this book, and Addison-Wesley was aware of a trademark claim, the designations have been printed with initial capital letters or in all capitals.

The authors and publisher have taken care in the preparation of this book, but make no expressed or implied warranty of any kind and assume no responsibility for errors or omissions. No liability is assumed for incidental or consequential damages in connection with or arising out of the use of the information or programs contained herein.

The publisher offers discounts on this book when ordered in quantity for special sales. For more information, please contact:

Pearson Education Corporate Sales Division
One Lake Street
Upper Saddle River, NJ 07458
(800) 382-3419
corpsales@pearsontechgroup.com

Visit AW on the Web: www.awprofessional.com

Library of Congress Cataloging-in-Publication Data

Jeffries, Ron,
    Extreme programming installed / Ron Jeffries, Ann Anderson, Chet Hendrickson.
        p.   cm.
    Includes bibliographical references and index
    ISBN 201-70842-6
    1. Computer software—Development.   I. Anderson, Ann
    II. Hendrickson, Chet.   III. Title.
    QA76.76.D47 J44 2000
    005.3—dc21

                                                                00–056928

ISBN 0-201-70842-6
This product is printed digitally on demand.

Fourth printing, April 2006

To Margaret, to Ron and Mike, to Ricia
—Ron

To my family
—Ann

To Sue
—Chet

Contents

Extreme Programming is a discipline of software development with values of simplicity, communication, feedback, and courage. We focus on the roles of customer, manager, and programmer and accord key rights and responsibilities to the people in those roles.

An XP project succeeds when the customers select business value to be implemented, based on the team's measured ability to deliver functionality over time.

An XP project needs a full-time customer to provide guidance. Here's a summary of why.

Define requirements with stories, written on cards.

- -

Here are some things we've paid a lot to learn. Since you bought the album, we wanted to give you a little something extra. Thank you, and we hope we passed the audition.

"We'll try" can be the saddest words a programmer has ever spoken, and most of us have spoken them more than once. We've covered this material in other forms already, but it bears repeating here.

Sometimes estimating stories seems scary. Keep your heads, stick together, and break the story down into small parts. You'll be surprised what you can do.

What about that database you need to build first? What about that framework? What about that syntax-directed command compiler? Get over it!

Are you looking for someone to blame? This chapter explains how to know whose fault it is. Now move on and solve your problems.

Those of you who have heard Ron, Ann, or me speak about XP are probably wondering where are all the war stories. Well, here's one.

An example showing how writing some tests can help you to improve the code.

Foreword

There are three things I like about this book (well, lots more than three, but I only have a foreword's worth of words to work with).

One: It's concrete. *Extreme Programming Explained* is a manifesto, a call to arms. "Hey gang, over there might not be so bad." The problem with manifestos, as history shows, is that execution of them is often fraught with difficulties (or outright impossibilities) that are not obvious from ten thousand meters away.

Extreme Programming Installed is all about really doing it—programming extreme. Here you will find a hundred little techniques for making the high-minded ideals of XP real and practical. And they are concrete, so you'll know from the first minute whether you are doing them or not.

Two: It's from experience. I had the great good fortune to work with Ron and Chet (and to a lesser extent with Ann) for an intense, frightening, challenging year at Chrysler. I learned a tremendous amount from them as we battled to figure out the details of delivering high-quality, high-value software. We had technical problems. We had people problems. We had management problems (and to be fair though, a whole lot of support). Our first year together was a microcosm of what can go wrong on a project. Software Engineering Reality 101.

Out of those experiences came a fountain of solutions. Funny, you put a team together and get most of the artificial obstacles out of their way, and you'll get good thoughts along the way to success. Since the C3 project at Chrysler, each of the authors has gone on to run extreme projects elsewhere. What you get in this book isn't a narrowly effective slice of practices, but rather the best of what worked for us there and elsewhere. When any technique in our field generates lots of press, charlatans and coat-tailers are bound to be close behind. We've already seen the fruits of the first consultants following the letter of XP but completely missing its spirit. XP Installed comes from folks who've done it, understood it, and expanded it.

Three: My friends wrote it. Don't get me wrong. I like writing books (witness *Planning Extreme Programming,* which I just finished writing with Martin Fowler). But I don't want to write them all. It would be the death of XP if I did write them all.

One of the failure scenarios for XP is if it turns into a cult of personality. "Sure this works for Kent, but thank goodness there's only one of him" is a charge leveled against XP by those who are afraid to try something different. *XP Installed* demonstrates that others can do XP, others can understand XP, and others can communicate about XP.

So, thanks, Ron and Chet and Ann, for writing this book. And reader, thanks for taking the time to read it and apply its principles. This book won't make your project for you. Only you can do that. But applying the lessons in these pages will make your project better.

—Kent Beck
Merlin, Oregon

Preface

How much would you pay for a software development team that would do what you want? Wait, don't answer yet—what if they could also tell you how much it would cost, so that you could decide what to do and what to defer, on your way to your deadline? You also get quality software, a robust array of tests that support the project through its entire lifecycle, and an up-to-date, clear view of project status. Best of all, you get the ability to change your mind about what you want, at any time.

There aren't any silver bullets in software development, and there probably never will be. However, Extreme Programming is a simple set of common-sense practices that, when used together, really can give you much of what you just read in the paragraph above. In this book, we tell you what the XP practices are, and how to install them in your project.

We are software developers. We have been involved in many successful projects, and even in some that weren't so successful. The successful ones were a lot more fun, for us, and for our customers. The unsuccessful ones have taught us a great deal about software development.

We have had the privilege of working on a great project, with a great teacher, Kent Beck. We helped shape the software process named Extreme Programming, XP for short. Since then, we have been helping everyone who will listen to learn from our experience.

The first book in the Extreme Programming series, *Extreme Programming Explained*, covers the reasoning behind the XP process. Based on our experience on the original XP project (and others), this book describes what makes XP work, day to day and month to month.

Successful software development is a team effort—not just the development team but the larger team consisting of customers, management, and developers. Extreme Programming is a simple process that brings these people together and helps them to succeed together. XP is aimed primarily at object-oriented projects using teams of a dozen or fewer programmers in one location. We would use XP for both in-house development and development of shrink-wrapped software. The principles of XP apply to any moderately sized project that needs to deliver quality software rapidly and flexibly.

XP is about balancing the needs of customers with the abilities of programmers, and about steering (managing the project to success). If you're a customer, a programmer, or a manager, here's what this book offers you:

Customers—who have software that needs to be developed: you will learn simple, effective ways to communicate what you need, to be sure that you are getting what you need, and to steer the project to success. You will learn that you can change your mind and still get what you need on time.

Programmers—who, on an XP project, define the architecture, design the system, and write the tests and the code that support them: you will learn how to deliver business value quickly, how to deal with changing requirements, and how to build customer confidence and support. You will learn to build for tomorrow by building only what you need today.

Managers—who control the project resources: you will learn how to measure project progress, how to measure quality, and how to answer the all-important question, "When will you be done?" You will learn an important truth of management—to use the programmers' actual performance to predict completion.

Customers, programmers, and managers must all work together to build the system that's needed. Chapter 1, *Extreme Programming*, will describe the roles, rights, and responsibilities, and provide a road map for the book. Dig right in. We're sure that the XP practices can improve your projects, as they have ours.

Acknowledgments

We all want to acknowledge our many reviewers, antagonists, and helpers from Wiki, the lists, the newsgroups, and real life. These include Vicki Abel, David Abernathy, Ken Auer, Brad Appleton, Boris Beizer,

Ed Berard, Bob Binder, Ken Boyer, Craig Brown, Tony Brown, Brian Button, Ian Chamberlain, Denis Clelland, Elliott Coates, Pascal Costanza, Randy Coulman, Bill Davis, Jutta Eckstein, Michael C. Feathers, Kim Freeborn, Sam Gentile, Gary Ham, Kay Hartman, Nathan Heagy, Stan Heckman, Dave Hendricksen, Robert Hirschfeld, Eric Hodges, Kaoru Hosokawa, Andrew Hunt, Jesper Rugaard Jensen, Ralph Johnson, Yutaka Kamite, Dierk König, Bob Koss, H. S. Lahman, A. Langton, Patrick Logan, Stephen Lozowski, Ross Macdonald, Ralph Mack, Robert C. Martin, Pete McBreen, Jim McFarland, Frank McGeough, Andrew McKinlay, Donald F. McLean, Erik Meade, Martijn Meijering, Peter Merel, John Merk, Eric Merrill, Gerard Meszaros, Chris Morris, George Nauman, Jim Newkirk, Will Nicholl, Tim Ottinger, Jeffrey Patton, Christian Pekeler, Mark Petersen, Philip C. (Phlip) Plumlee, Nick Pratt, Dan Rawsthorne, Gareth Reeves, Matthias Ressel, Jim Roepcke, Jakob Røjel, Doug Rosenberg, Steven Salter, Robert Schaefer, Paul Sinnett, Andreas Sjöstedt, Dan Sketcher, Anne Smigelsky, Stefan Steurs, Dr. Oliver Strebel, Doug Swartz, Dave Thomas, Dominic Twyman, Bill Watkins, Sarah Weaver, Trevor Weiman, Don Wells, Frank Westphal, Trevor Wieman, Mark Windholtz, Tim Woodard, Rick Zaccone, Barry Zhao. If your name isn't here and should be, we apologize sincerely. You, and many others have all helped us make this a better book. Mistakes, of course, are Chet's fault.

The Addison-Wesley team, Mike Hendrickson, Heather Peterson, John Fuller, and Maggie Carr got us into this and got us out alive. Thanks!

And special thanks to Jennifer Kohnke for the pictures!

Jennifer

Ron

First, thanks to Kent Beck, whose phone call began five of the most interesting, exciting, and educational years of a life that has been full of such years. To Ward Cunningham, whose patient teaching makes me think that one day I may learn something, and who leaves me in awe most every time we meet. To Alistair Cockburn, for explaining to me what I'm doing. And to Martin Fowler, for advice, honesty, and keeping me on the straight and narrow.

Over the years there have been so many to thank: mentors like Morris Dansky and Tom Donohue; benefactors like Rick Camp, Rick Crandall, Dov Weizman, Mark Roth, Charlie O'Rourke, and Don Devine; a near infinite array of wonderful coworkers like Steve Weiss, Gene Somdahl, Charles Bair, Rick Evarts, Mike McConnell, Jean Musinski, Karen Dueweke, Dave Childs, Gregg Cieslak, and of course the whole C3 team, whom Chet lists below. So many others: I could fill the book. And Bill Rogers, for the FORTRAN manual.

Ann and Chet helped more than they know. Their words, their energy, and their organization pervade this book. Honestly, it could not have been done without them.

Mom and Dad, Margaret and Ron Jeffries, gave me life itself and what I sometimes think was the only normal home life in the universe. They gave me my brothers, Dick, Tom, and Patrick, who bring love, concern, and humor all together.

Thanks to my sons Ron and Mike for showing me what joyful excellence our chosen work can be. Guys, you make me proud, and humble.

My wife Ricia has tolerated nearly every stupid thing I've done over many years now and has supported my strange late leap into independence and Extreme Programming with hardly a whimper. She has also tolerated my vehicle habit. Thank you, Ricia.

Ann

The first person I want to acknowledge is Ron Jeffries. He has been a mentor, as well as a good friend, for most of my adult life. Ron also did most of the writing for this book; without him, this book would not exist. Thank you, Ron, for all of your work and all of your time.

Next, I want to thank Kent Beck. Kent is the person who took the values and practices that make up Extreme Programming and gave them a name. Alone, that would have been a really good start, but he took the concept of Extreme Programming even further. He wrote a book, talked about it with anyone who would listen, and made Extreme Programming visible (and interesting) to the technical community. Thank you, Kent, for the vision and the reality.

I would also like to thank my coworkers, past and present. The people you work with can make a huge difference in how much you enjoy your work. The people I've worked with have been, and continue to be, wonderful. Some of the people that deserve special mention are Gregg Cieslak, Don Devine, Jim Howe, Bob Simms, Madhu Bhangi, the C3 team (listed by Chet below), and Charlie O'Rourke.

Finally, I want to thank my family. I got my love of learning from my father, George Anderson. My mother, Elsie Schmutzler, gave me my work ethic, persistence, and determination. My grandmother, Rose Anderson, is a role model. My siblings, Amy Olson, Aaron Anderson, and Alan Anderson, are my friends. The little people in my life, Kirsten and Kali, show me joy in simple pleasures. All of you have given many gifts, but the most precious is your love. Thank you.

Chet

I would like to thank Ron Jeffries, not only for letting me work on his book, but for all the things he has taught me about software development, from coding-by-intention to how to communicate with the CIO.

The story we tell in this book is mostly the story of what we learned on the Chrysler Consolidated Compensation (C3) project. Tom Hadfield was able to bring together a group of smart, dedicated, and skilled people to make C3 happen. Thanks, Tom, for letting me work on your project. XP is all about trusting the customers to know what they need and when they need it. C3 had the prototype for XP customers—Marie DeArment. Marie made us do the right thing; thank you, Marie. The whole C3 team deserves congratulations for helping to make Extreme Programming what it is. They are Ann Anderson, Ed Anderi, Ralph Beattie, Kent Beck, David Bryant, Bob Coe, Marie DeArment, Martin Fowler, Margaret Fronczak, Rich Garzaniti, Dennis Gore, Brian Hacker, Ron Jeffries, Doug Joppie, David Kim, Paul Kowalsky, Debbie Mueller, Tom Murasky, Richard Nutter, Adrian Pantea, Matt Saigeon, Susan Smythe, Ciro Vitale, Don Thomas, and Don Wells.

Thank you to my parents, Bill and Joan Hendrickson. Without their support and understanding I would never have gotten here. I also would like to acknowledge Paul Lewis's role in helping to kindle my lifelong curiosity. And most importantly, I must thank my wife, Sue Hendrickson, for her love and understanding, for her encouragement and support, and for all that she is.

Chapter 1

Extreme Programming

Extreme Programming is a discipline of software development with values of simplicity, communication, feedback, and courage. We focus on the roles of customer, manager, and programmer and accord key rights and responsibilities to the people in those roles.

The Customer Role

The customer chooses what will deliver business value, chooses what to do first and what to defer, and defines the tests to show that the system does what it needs to.

Every software project needs to deliver business value. To be successful, the team needs to build the right things, in the right order, and to be sure that what they build actually works. Of course, this can't be done without programmers,[1] but in fact the customer's role is critical in steering that process to success.

The customer role on an XP project can be filled by one person, or by several. The team will be most effective if the customer stays on-site and present with the team, full-time. We'll discuss some details in *On-Site Customer* (page 17). Here, we'll talk in more general terms about what the customer does. If you're the XP customer, we're talking to you.

Note that we say "the customer" and not "the customers." Whether they are one person or many people, the XP customer always speaks with one voice. The determination of what will have business value, and the order of building that value, rests solely with the customer. (Don't worry, you get lots of help and advice. But ultimately, you get to make the call.)

An XP team plans and builds software in terms of "stories." Stories are just that—individual stories about how the system needs to work. Each story describes one thing that the system needs to do. Each story must be understood well enough that the programmers can estimate its difficulty. And each story must be testable.

As the customer, you express what must be done in terms of stories. For a project spanning a few months, there may be 50 or 100 stories. Larger projects of course have more stories. We'll talk more about the details in *User Stories* (page 23).

You probably have a delivery date in mind, though some projects have a fixed feature list rather than a fixed date. We are not content to imagine that everything that you can think of will be done by a given date. Neither should you be. Instead, the XP process lets the team predict, more and more accurately, how much work can be done in any given time period. Using this information, you manage project scope—choosing what to do now and what to defer until later—to ensure successful delivery.

---

1. In this book the pronouns "he" and "she" are used randomly to reflect the broad diversity that makes our industry great.

You, the customer, have the critical responsibility to choose the stories that will provide the most valuable features, the highest business value, and that can be accomplished by the desired delivery date. The XP development process lets you choose among the stories with great flexibility. There's not much limitation on what can be done first and what second. This is by design; if you are to choose the stories for successful on-time release, you must have the flexibility to make the choice as independently as possible. Read more about this process in *Customer Defines Release* (page 55) and *Iteration Planning* (page 61).

Finally, you specify tests that show whether the stories have been correctly implemented. These *Acceptance Tests* (page 31), whether built by the programmers, by an independent tester, or by you—the customers—yourselves, provide confidence that the system really does what it needs to do.

Define business value, decide what to do and what to defer, and define the tests to show that the system works. These are your key responsibilities as the XP customer.

The Programmer Role

The programmers analyze, design, test, program, and integrate the system. The programmers estimate the difficulty of all stories, and track the pace at which they can deliver stories to the customer.

If the project is to deliver business value, each story must be understood. Software must be designed, tested, and built to implement that story, and all the software must be brought together into a coherent whole. That is the XP programmer's job. If you're the XP programmer, we're talking to you.

In Extreme Programming, the emphasis is on programming. Everything we do looks like programming and is focused on the most critical artifact of software development, the program.

Build the system in small releases, so that the customer benefit is maximized and you get the best possible feedback on how you're doing. We talk about this in *Small Releases* (page 49), *Customer Defines Release* (page 55), and *Iteration Planning* (page 61).

Base the program on simple, clear design. This lets you produce quality software quickly. There's more discussion of this in *Code Quality* (page 83), and *A True Story* (page 225). As you learn more about what the design wants to be, improve the design using *Refactoring* (page 76).

XP is neither slash and burn, nor code and fix programming. Not at all. Extreme Programming is about careful and continuous design, rapid feedback from extensive testing, and the maintenance of relentlessly clear and high-quality code.

Keep the system integrated at all times, so there's always a good version to look at. Keeping integrated lets you go rapidly without stepping on each others' toes. See *Continuous Integration* (page 78).

Share the ownership of all the code, so no one has to wait and everyone feels able to make everything better. See *Collective Code Ownership* (page 75), and *Releasing Changes* (page 121). Share a single *Coding Standard* (page 79) as well, whether self-evolved or adopted from elsewhere. Make everyone's code look alike—it helps with communication and team focus. Express individuality in the way you wear your XP ball cap, not in your code.

Make sure that the system always works, using comprehensive unit tests that you write, as well as the customer's acceptance tests. These tests allow rapid change and support collective code ownership by keeping change from introducing mistakes. See *Unit Tests* (page 93), *Acceptance Tests* (page 31), *Everything That Could Possibly Break* (page 233), and *Test First, by Intention* (page 107).

Write all production code in pairs, for maximum speed and cross-training, in support of shared code ownership and rapid progress, as described in *Pair Programming* (page 87).

Extreme Programming is an approach to software development that lets programmers do what they do best—program—while giving the customers what they need most—business value. It's a win-win approach and fun, too.

The Manager Role

The manager brings the customer and developers together and helps them meld into a smoothly operating team. You don't do the process—you make the process smoother.

If you're the XP manager, we're talking to you. The XP process specifies how the team does certain things that conventional managers sometimes do. But don't worry—there's plenty for the XP project manager to do. On an XP project, the manager's role is key, and it is very much focused on management per se.

The first and last job of a good manager is to get things out of the way of the people who are doing the work. Look for things that are slowing the team, and use your special managerial powers to resolve them. Expedite purchases, make sure the workspace is arranged effectively, keep the computers up-to-date, lean on the LAN guys to fix problems, and so on. A manager's success depends on removing everything from the team's path that doesn't contribute to the objective of delivering good software on time.

When it comes to the day-to-day process of planning, designing, testing, coding, releasing, managers don't do any of these things directly. However, you do something more important: You cause these things to be done, coordinate their doing, and report the results.

It may seem that the entire team just magically appears at the planning table when it's time for the next release plan. It's not magic; it's your doing.

As manager, you cause that meeting to happen, and you coordinate it into existence. At a stand-up meeting a bit before release planning time, mention the need for the meeting and suggest a date. If there's general agreement, go ahead. If there are scheduling conflicts, go around to the team members and find a suitable date and time. If necessary, encourage someone to change a conflicting appointment.

When the date is chosen, prepare the ground. Arrange a room, send out the invitations, order the refreshments, or cause these things to be done if you have administrative help.

Before any planning meeting, check with the customers, reminding them to be ready and to bring any new stories, and so on. If they need help, provide it.

If necessary, coordinate or facilitate each meeting—or designate someone to do so. Help to keep the team on process, make notes on the proceedings, offer to get special resource people if they're needed, and so on.

After each meeting, if reporting needs to be done, do it or cause it to be done. (Internal reporting generally is not needed. The plan is on the white board and in the minds of the team. But keep some stakeholders outside the room up-to-date.)

During the iteration, it's the same: cause the right things to happen, coordinate the activities, report results, and always remove obstacles.

The project manager usually has responsibility for personnel and this is a very important one. Even on the best teams, there are differences between individuals, and sometimes there can be temporary or permanent people problems.

When people have a conflict, you need to fix it. If someone's behavior is harming the team, you have to address the problem. If the individual cannot or will not correct the behavior, you must remove him or her from the team. This should not be done lightly or precipitously, but sometimes it must be done, and it is the project manager's responsibility.

There can sometimes be political problems that impact the team. These are major obstacles and the manager leaps in to resolve them. A stakeholder may have difficulty allowing the customer to schedule the stories or may put pressure on the programmers to adjust their estimates. Watch for outside forces that can impact your team and, when needed, firmly and productively step in.

On the good side, the project manager gets to give rewards. There is the annual rating and salary adjustment ritual. We can't tell you how to do this—extreme teams are all over the map on compensation policy. It's the manager's responsibility to have fair and consistent assessments of the staff and to have compensation fairly reflect those assessments.

And think about small rewards as well. Recognition is important. New toys or tokens for the team. A round of Laser Tag, a round of beers, a night at the opera. A little time off from work and off the books. And don't forget the families.

This only scratches the surface. The project manager's role is very important to the project. If done creatively and effectively, it can greatly ensure the team's success.

Cause, coordinate, report, and reward. And always: remove obstacles.

Rights and Responsibilities

Extreme Programming tries to provide certain benefits to the managers, customers, and developers involved in a project. We express these as rights because they are very important to the success of the project and to the team members.

Manager and Customer Rights

1. You have the right to an overall plan, to know what can be accomplished, when, and at what cost.
2. You have the right to get the most value out of every programming week.
3. You have the right to see progress in a running system, proven to work by passing repeatable tests that you specify.
4. You have the right to change your mind, to substitute functionality, and to change priorities without paying exorbitant costs.
5. You have the right to be informed of schedule changes, in time to choose how to reduce scope to restore the original date. You can cancel at any time and be left with a useful working system reflecting investment to date.

Programmer Rights

1. You have the right to know what is needed, with clear declarations of priority.
2. You have the right to produce quality work at all times.
3. You have the right to ask for and receive help from peers, superiors, and customers.
4. You have the right to make and update your own estimates.
5. You have the right to accept your responsibilities instead of having them assigned to you.

This book is about helping your project deliver these rights. Here's a bit of discussion about why each of these proposed rights is beneficial to a successful software project, and how XP helps to provide that benefit.

You Have the Right to an Overall Plan, to Know What Can Be Accomplished, When, and at What Cost

For the project to be guided to success, it's necessary to know overall what is needed and what can be accomplished within the time and budget available. *User Stories* (page 23) describes how we use stories to define the product. *Small Releases* (page 49) ensures that you can learn what you need to know before time runs out. *Customer Defines Release* (page 55) describes how you build and maintain an overall view of the project.

You Have the Right to Get the Most Value Out of Every Programming Week

Having a plan isn't everything, but planning is. Project time is short, and you need to be sure that the right things are happening every week. *Iteration Planning*, page 61, describes XP's short-range planning component.

You Have the Right to See Progress in a Running System, Proven to Work by Passing Repeatable Tests that You Specify

Real management comes from having concrete information. In addition to delivering frequently with *Small Releases* (page 49), an XP project keeps the system built at all times (*Continuous Integration*, page 78), and uses tests provided by the customer to show the customer that the system really works (*Acceptance Tests*, page 31).

You Have the Right to Change Your Mind, to Substitute Functionality, and to Change Priorities without Paying Exorbitant Costs

Things change. Market requirements change, and business requirements change. An XP project thrives on change, through simple design, kept simple through *Refactoring* (page 76). By allowing for change, we give the customer the best chance to guide the project to success.

You Have the Right to Be Informed of Schedule Changes, in Time to Choose How to Reduce Scope to Restore the Original Date. You Can Cancel at Any Time and Be Left with a Useful Working System Reflecting Investment to Date

Too often, projects get to 90 percent done and stay there with no real information coming out. Then there's a sudden huge slip near the end. XP works to be sure that everyone knows just what is really happening, with clear and honest reporting (*Resources, Scope, Quality, Time*, page 135), as well as the public Acceptance Tests. Because an XP project implements business value first, and because of *Small Releases* (page 49) and *Continuous Integration* (page 78), the product can be kept always ready for release.

You Have the Right to Know What Is Needed, with Clear Declarations of Priority

Programmers want to implement what is really needed, but things get in the way. Sometimes they don't understand what is needed; user stories, described in *User Stories* (page 23), help with that. And sometimes programmers don't understand what is really important to the business. XP programmers work on business value, as directed by the customers, described in *Customer Defines Release* (page 55) and *Iteration Planning* (page 61).

You Have the Right to Produce Quality Work at All Times

Programmers want to do good work. XP practices ensure good work while delivering business value. Contributing topics include *Unit Tests* (page 93), as well as *Refactoring* (page 76) and *Simple Design*. Another XP core practice, *Pair Programming* (page 87), improves quality, improves time to delivery, and even provides cross-training among the staff.

You Have the Right to Ask for and Receive Help from Peers, Superiors, and Customers

Sometimes programmers get buried in the complexity of their work. Help from colleagues and managers can speed things up and get things back on track. In XP, we recommend an *On-Site Customer* (page 17) to be sure that requirements are understood. We use *Pair Programming* (page 87) to provide constant help. We offer some additional support techniques when we discuss the *The Manager Role* (page 4). But the fundamental rule is this: No one can ever refuse to help a team member who needs help.

You Have the Right to Make and Update Your Own Estimates

The most critical factor in the success of your project is knowing when you are going to be done. By knowing how long it will really take—not just how long you *hope* it will take—you can guide the project to success by managing what is worked on. XP's *Customer Defines Release* (page 55) and *Iteration Planning* (page 61) allow you to do that management. Having the programmers do *Story Estimation* (page 37) gives you the information you need to steer the planning.

You Have the Right to Accept Your Responsibilities Instead of Having Them Assigned to You

We all work most effectively when we have accepted our responsibilities instead of having them thrust upon us. Part of the ritual of the XP *Iteration Planning* (page 61) is that programmers sign up for what they will work on. At that time, they choose to do the work and put their name down for what they will accomplish. This small act of commitment engages the individual's own honor as a necessary part of the team.

Project Flow

The rest of the book follows the chronological flow of an XP project. We've pointed to many of the chapters earlier in this introduction. An XP project begins with an on-site customer, who provides the stories that define the system, and the acceptance tests that prove the system works. We focus on small releases, each one defined by the customer. We work in short iterations, again working on the customer's stories of highest business value.

Programmers follow a number of important practices, including *Simple Design* (page 75), *Refactoring* (page 76), *Collective Code Ownership* (page 75), and *Pair Programming* (page 87). They write their code including extensive *Unit Tests* (page 93), ensuring consistent progress and high quality.

Based on the early iterations, the team uses *Experience Improves Estimates* (page 131) to predict future performance, which sets the project up for success through constant informed *Steering* (page 147).

There will be a few defects (no one is perfect), and we'll tell you how to deal with them in *Handling Defects* (page 161).

Finally, we include some *Bonus Tracks* (page 175), essays and ideas we couldn't bear to leave out even though they don't exactly fit in the chronological flow. We paid a lot to learn those things, and we wanted to share them with you. So dive in and check out *Extreme Programming Installed*!

Chapter 2

The Circle of Life

An XP project succeeds when the customers select business value to be implemented, based on the team's measured ability to deliver functionality over time.

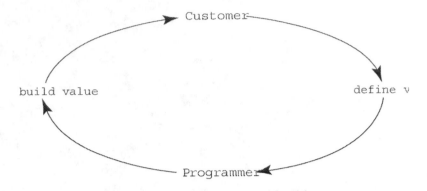

FIGURE 2.1 Customer defines, programmer builds

Steering a project to success all comes down to what we call the "circle of life." The customer's basic job is to define what has value, and the programmer's job is to build it (see Figure 2.1).

On an XP project, the customer defines business value by writing stories, and the programmer implements those stories, building business value. But there's an important caveat: on an XP project, the programmers do what the customer asks them to do!

Business value depends on what you get, on when you get it, and how much it costs. To decide what to do, and when, the customers need to know the cost of what they ask for. The programmers, based on experience, provide this information. Then the customers choose what they want, and the programmers build it. Now the picture looks like Figure 2.2.

Every time we go around the circle, we learn. Customers learn how valuable their proposed features really are, while programmers learn how difficult those features really are. We all learn how long it really takes to build the features we need (see Figure 2.3).

We hate to be the ones to break this to you, but some things are probably going to take longer than you'd like. The good news is that you can inform yourself about how fast you're going, and you can use that information to choose the best mix of features for each release. By managing scope, you can schedule good, solid releases for the dates you need.

The best way to get a good release by a given date is to know how fast the programmers are delivering features, and to use that knowledge

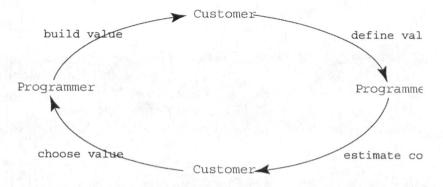

FIGURE 2.2 Programmer estimates, customer chooses

to choose the best mix of features possible by your chosen date. You must manage the scope of your project.

It's tempting to put pressure on the programmers, to "hold their feet to the fire," in hopes of getting more done. If you want your software written by people who are under stress because their feet are on fire, do this. If you want quality to take a back seat, do this. To get the best possible combination of features, with the quality you need, you must manage scope.

It's tempting to believe your own wishes, or your own press releases, and schedule more work than measurement says you will do. If you want to ship late, do this. If you want to ship on time, but with

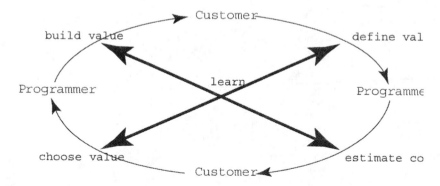

FIGURE 2.3 Improve estimates of value and cost

a random collection of buggy features, do this. For a predictable delivery, with the quality you need, you must manage scope.

The circle of life is profoundly important. When customers and programmers recognize that they depend on each other, the team can steer the project so that there's always the most business value implemented at any given moment. The upcoming chapters will show you how to get the stories that define the product, estimate story cost with increasing precision, track how you're doing, and select the stories for a successful release.

If what you want to do is manage your project to the most successful conclusion, then follow the circle of life: define, estimate, choose, build. And learn.

Chapter 3

On-Site Customer

An XP project needs a full-time customer to provide guidance.
Here's a summary of why.

Programmers, we all know, will program anything. The trick is to tell them what's needed. In general, what's needed is called "requirements," probably to make it sound more important. In XP, we communicate what's needed using *User Stories* (page 23). User stories, written on cards, are the core of the XP planning process (see Chapters 8 and 9), and they belong to the people with the requirements. We call these people the Customer—and we ask them to be with the project all the time. Before you read about creating user stories, here's why we want you to show up.

The essence of what makes an XP project successful was described in *The Circle of Life* (page 13). The project is *steered* to success by the customer and programmers working in concert. An XP team wants to go as fast as possible, and the XP value of simplicity contributes strongly to that goal. Written specifications take a long time to write, and they don't communicate very well. It's much more effective to have conversations about what is needed as the project goes along.

Not every project can afford this, and other projects' members fear that they can't. But the plain truth is that the more time the customer and programmers spend together, the better things go. That doesn't mean that the customer is holding the programmers' hands, but it does mean that being immediately available to answer questions is of immense value.

There are many studies that show that communication is reduced hugely by separation. Moving coworkers one floor down reduces communication almost as much as moving them across the world. Communication, of course, is another of the XP values. You want your project to be successful, so of course you want everyone communicating. The programmers will communicate with each other, primarily through *Pair Programming* (page 87). Communication between the customer and programmer occurs during *Customer Defines Release* (page 55), and *Iteration Planning* (page 61). Frankly, we need more. The planning process works efficiently through writing user stories on cards and using those cards in planning. The stories, though, are promissory notes, redeemable for conversations about the details of the requirements.

A simple story may need backup details that can be provided on paper. But for the programmers to implement the story quickly and well, they need to build up a sense of how it fits in. That sense is provided by the customer, in many discussions, over the course of the project. Here's an example:

> *Union dues vary by union and are taken only in the first pay period of the month. The system computes the deduction automatically. The amount is shown in the attached table.*

Attached to this story, the programmer might find a small spreadsheet showing the various unions and their dues. She notices that there are two line items for members of UPGWA (you-PIG-wa), the United Plant Guard Workers of America. The items are labeled "Tier 1" and "Tier 2." She goes to the customer and asks,

> "What's the deal on plant guards, tier one and tier two?"
>
> "The agreement with the union divides plant guards into two groups," the customer replies, "called Tier One and Tier Two. The two tiers have different dues rates and benefits."
>
> "How do I tell them apart?"
>
> "It's all by date of hire. All plant guards hired after September 1995 are Tier Two."
>
> "OK, got it. By the way, are those dues figures you gave us solid for all time?"
>
> "No way," laughs the customer. "Next time there's a union negotiation, those figures will all change. There's a story coming up giving us the ability to change them. For now, just put them in that way."
>
> "OK, thanks," says the programmer, and returns to her desk in less time than it took to read this.

Now yes, that same exchange could have been held via e-mail, or written down in a detailed spec. But that would have taken more time, and quite likely wouldn't have completely quelled the programmer's concern the way the conversation did. You might also be concerned that this important information about the requirements will get lost somewhere, but remember that you will have specified acceptance tests, and they will surely cover the two tiers of plant guards.

You could perhaps get this much certainty by writing more down. But you would have to write lots more, which would slow the project and still not obviate the need for conversation. With an on-site customer, you save time and trees, and build a rapport between the customer and the programmers that serves to help you over any tough times that may come along.

How important is it to have the customer right there? Here's an example. Ron has been coaching a project whose customers have a private office right in the development area. A couple of times every day, while the programmers are working, one of them will ask a question and no one will know the answer. The programmer generally gets right up and goes to ask Pam, the customer. In a couple of minutes, he's back, shares the answer (because now everyone is curious), and gets back to work.

One day on Ron's last visit, the customers had to go to another work site for machine access. They told the programmers where they were (two floors down and a few offices over), and left their phone number and beeper number. Sure enough, in the afternoon, someone had one of those questions. But the programmer knew Pam wasn't there. He didn't call her—instead, he guessed about the code and wrote a note to ask her later.

How many guesses do you want in your code? How many times do you want programmers working on lower priority work while they wait for an answer on what you have set as the highest priority? Where possible, keep a customer with the programmers. You'll be glad you did.

On-Site Customers Do Real Work

Sometimes you can't afford to have the customer removed from doing real customer-related work. That's fine—Pam and her partner Robin have real jobs, too. They're set up with computer access in the programming area, and one or the other of them is usually there. They mostly do their regular work and answer a few questions. Their answers make the relocation worthwhile.

If the Customer Can't Be There

Sometimes the customer really is too valuable to be on-site. Stock traders are thought to fall into this group. Sometimes, the customer is in a different city from the programmers. This happens in many companies, and there's no way either customers or programmers are moving. Well, you're going to pay a price, but here are some tips on what to do.

First, try hard to get someone to represent the customer locally. This could be a non-programming project manager, a trainer, a tracker, or just someone in the company who is expert in the area. Let them handle the bulk of the interruptions, then get with the real customer off-line to double-check. If the customer and this pseudo-customer can get on the same wavelength, this works quite well.

Second, at least try to get the real customer on-site for planning meetings. In those meetings there is lots of discussion about priorities, and it's really best if the real customer makes those trade-offs. This is also a good chance for the pseudo-customer to get re-synchronized with the real one.

Third, visit the customer. Send the programmers—all of them, if you can—to visit the customer as often as possible. Ask questions, discuss the application, and build rapport.

Fourth, release code very frequently to the real customer. If they can't see you, make sure that they see the system. You'll be releasing rapidly anyway, being an XP team, but the need for this is higher if your customer isn't around, and the frequency should go up.

Fifth, expect misunderstandings and plan for them. The written and e-mail communications you'll fall back on are error-prone, not because you are bad people but because that's how it is with the written word. Plan frequent phone conferences and meetings, to settle issues and to remind everyone that even though they aren't together, they're all part of the same team.

Summary

Having your customer with you is really valuable. It's possible to survive without it—many projects do—but you'll go faster and more smoothly by being together. It's the difference between being in the car when it's time to turn or just writing a note that says, "Don't forget to turn at 34th Street." When 34th is blocked and you're in the car, you can tell the driver how to recover. The note can't help.

Somewhere along the way in your project, 34th Street will be blocked, and having the customer there will bring the project back on line so smoothly it'll be as if it never happened. And every day, the small conversations will add up to a lot of trust and communication between customers and programmers. That, of course, leads to success.

Chapter 4

User Stories

Define requirements with stories, written on cards.

Customers have the right to get the most possible value out of every programming moment, by asking for small atomic bits of functionality. Programmers have the right to know what is needed. These two rights come together in the user story.

Each user story is a short description of the behavior of the system, from the point of view of the user of the system. In XP, the system is specified entirely through stories.

Analysis can be loosely described as the process of finding out what the customer wants. Analysis can be done very formally, with objects and diagrams, or it can be done very informally. XP, no surprise, chooses informal analysis: we ask the customer.

It should also be no surprise that we don't limit analysis to the beginning of the project—what we call drive-by analysis. In XP, you do analysis all the time. The user story is the medium of analysis—the medium of communication between the customer and the programmer.

XP recognizes that the customer will be learning what is needed, based on what has been done so far. By keeping stories small, releasing often, and bringing customer and programmer together, the XP approach to analysis ensures that what is learned can be fed back into the development process, making the final result as close as possible to what is really needed.

Starting with Stories

Your XP analysis kit is a pack of blank cards. Four by six or 5×8 unlined cards are about right. Experiment a little, but you'll probably wind up wanting to use only one size card throughout your project. They're easier to handle in bulk if they're all the same size. And get lots—we use them for everything, and we like to tear them up.

You'll need a comfortable space where a couple of customers and a couple of programmers can sit at a table and work. Use your planning table or any other convenient spot. Customer and programmer sitting side by side, not across the table, works best.

Unwrap the cards. They're hard to use in the plastic wrap. And the unwrapping is the hardest part of the process. Whew, glad that's over.

Now, hand everyone some cards. We each take one card to test our pen on. We each scribble something on our card. Now—we each tear up our card![1] This gets us all in the frame of mind to touch the cards, write on them, and be flexible, ripping up and replacing cards whenever need be.

---

1. Thanks to Erik Meade for this technique! Sometimes you'll have a player who resists tearing up his card. Watch for other signs of inflexibility, and find ways to help him relax into the process. But don't touch his cards!

The first few story cards are a bit difficult. But don't worry, you've got lots of blank cards to use. Customer, tell a story about how the system will be used. Programmers, listen and ask questions for understanding. Try to stay away from implementation questions. Now, customer, write the story, in your own words, on a single card. If the whole story is too big, write the essential core.

As you go through this process, especially with helpful questions, you'll often decide that a story you've written isn't quite right. That's great. Tear that card up and make a new one.

This is very important: Analysis on cards is flexible. It's not just OK to tear up a card and start a new one—it's the best thing that can happen! Tear up cards early and often, so that everyone gets good at it.

Sample Stories

Here are some sample stories. Each one is backed up with conversation (see *Stories Are Promises for Conversation*, page 28). Each has related detailed information. Each one is simple enough that the programmers can understand it and can see how to implement it in a week or so.

Union dues vary by union and are taken only in the first pay period of the month. The system computes the deduction automatically. The amount is shown in the attached table.

When a transaction causes a customer's account to go into overdraft, transfer money from the overdraft protection account, if any.

When a transaction causes a customer's account to go into overdraft, send an e-mail showing the transaction and balance to the customer. If overdraft protection is in effect, show the overdraft transaction and the resulting account balances in the e-mail.

For each account, compute the balance by adding up all the deposits and subtracting all the deductions.

Produce a statement for each account, showing transaction date, number, payee, and amount. A sample statement is attached—make the report look approximately like the sample.

Each employee may be subject to one or more legally mandated wage attachments. The KBS application Wage-Attach accepts on-line inquiries on whether an EE has an attachment, and if so, the payee and amount. Make each deduction, and send a message to the Attachment Payment System authorizing the transfer to the payee. (Programmer note: don't know enough to estimate—we need to do an experiment. Story may need splitting.)

When the GPS has contact with two or fewer satellites for more than 60 seconds, it should display the message "Poor satellite contact," and wait for confirmation from the user. If contact improves before confirmation, clear the message automatically.

If the station currently playing carries digital information, the information is displayed in the radio's LCD display. If there is no digital information available, display the station frequency.

Allow the user to add new service types to the system's initial list. For example, he may wish to add a special entry for getting the car washed at the high school's "free" wash. Include the standard fields amount and date, plus allow the user to add any additional text or numeric fields. Reports should automatically sum any numeric fields. (Programmer note: story needs splitting. Please separate text and numeric fields into two stories, plus one for the summing.)

(Split 1) Allow the user to add new service types, including the standard fields plus any additional text fields desired.

(Split 2) Allow the user to add numeric fields to user-defined service types.

(Split 3) In all reports, show totals of all numeric fields, not just the standard gallons and dollar amount fields.

For most of the stories above, the programmers (the authors) could see how to implement them in a week or less. As such, we felt that we understood the stories and could implement them. In the case of the last story, we felt that adding special numeric fields might be difficult, and that updating all the reports to include them was a separate effort and might take a long time. We asked that the customer split the story, and the customer agreed.

Note that we'd really get the story split in a conversation with the customer explaining what was up—not just with a note on the card. We put the note in the text because we can't have a conversation with you. In a real XP project, use conversation wherever you can.

Stories Are Promises for Conversation[2]

User stories are made up of two components. The written card is the first. We recommend writing the story in just a couple of sentences on a

---

2. Alistair Cockburn gave us this elegant description of story as promise for conversation. Buy his books!

card and pointing to any supporting documentation. The second component, and by far the most important, is the series of conversations that will take place between the customer and the programmers over the life of the story. These conversations will be captured as additional documentation that will be attached to the story, will be acted out during Class Responsibility Collaborator (CRC) design sessions, and, better yet, as acceptance tests and application code.

Each story card is carried through the project, serving as a token for planning and implementing whatever it requests. As such, the programmers need to be able to make a decent estimate of how difficult each story is, usually in small numbers of weeks of effort. Just how big a story can be varies from project to project. The best way to begin is just to write a few stories and ask the programmers if they are the right size and detail.

Do Programmers Ever Write Stories?

It's better if programmers don't write stories. We want all the stories to belong to the customer, not just in name but in their heart. There are some times when the programmers may help the customer write the stories. For example, if the customer doesn't know how to write stories, the programmers may need to work with her to find out what the system needs to do. These conversations become the stories. It may seem that you know something the customer will want. Talk with the customer about it, but resist the temptation to write the stories. XP depends on the circle of life, with the customer defining and the programmer building. Don't break the circle.

It may seem that there is some large technical development that needs to be scheduled and managed. Some teams do write these as "technical stories," but this also threatens the circle. Customers can't prioritize what they don't understand, and all too often the technical bite is too big to fit into a single iteration. Where possible—and it usually is—you should solve this by relating the technical task back to a real customer need, and breaking it down into iteration-size bites.

How Many Stories Do You Need?

It depends on the complexity of the system. A more complex system will need more stories; a simpler system will need fewer. There should be at least one story for every major feature in the system. Here's a rule of thumb: you'll probably need at least one story per programmer per month. Two would be better. So if you have ten people for six months, that's between 60 and 120 stories. If you have fewer than that, stories will probably need to be split. If you have more, that can be OK; this is just a rule of thumb. The most important thing is to get as many of the stories as soon as possible. Then estimate them as described in *Story Estimation* (page 37).

Can Stories Be Too Big or Too Small?

For planning purposes, stories should encompass a week or two of programmer time. We pick that number to give the customer good control over scope, but also because programmer estimates are pretty good over that range of time. When a programmer looks at a story, rolls his eyes, and mumbles, "Uh, that might be a month, maybe six weeks," we are pretty sure he doesn't really know how to do it. So we ask the customer to split the story.

It's usually easy to break a big story down into two or more smaller ones. Often the story has a very important part and a less important part: That's a good place to split. Other times the story covers several related cases: Consider making each one a story. Customers, don't worry about not getting everything. You can select all of these stories for implementation if you want to. We just need to break them down into bite-sized chunks for estimation.

Other times, stories will be too small. When stories get estimates of just a couple of days or less, they can gum up the planning process. It's best to clip related stories together and estimate them as a group. Use your own judgment here, but if the planning seems to slow down, or becomes very rote, it may be time to put some stories into a group.

What if You Don't Have All the Stories?

Don't worry—you don't have all the stories. Things will change and new ideas will come to you. You can substitute stories at the beginning of any iteration. Just get the programmers to estimate them, and stick them into the planning process when their cost and value dictate. Grab a few cards, write down the new stories, and act like you had them all the time. No one will ever notice.

What's the Next Step with Stories?

Thanks for asking. That's the next chapter called *Acceptance Tests*.

Chapter 5

Acceptance Tests

Surely you aren't going to assume you're getting what you need. Prove that it works! Acceptance tests allow the customer to know when the system works and tell the programmers what needs to be done.

Customers, remember that you have the right to see progress in the form of a working system, passing repeatable tests that you specify. Well, here's the responsibility part of that: specifying the acceptance tests.

Every system undergoes testing to find out whether it works as needed. Some don't get this testing until they go into use and actual users discover flaws for themselves. This leads to pain; pain leads to hatred; hatred leads to suffering. Don't do that—test before you ship.

Some systems put off overall testing until right before release. They often eat into the testing time with schedule overruns, but even if they allocate the full testing period, this slows things down. The reason is simple: programmers forget what they did. If I write a program today and test it a week from now, my recollection of how I wrote it will have faded, in favor of whatever I'm working on then. So, when I get the defect indication, I won't be able to guess quickly where the problem is. This leads to long debugging sessions, and slows the project down. Don't do that—test right away.

XP values feedback, and there is no more important feedback than early information on how well the program works. If it were possible to have the computer beep at the programmer one second after she made a mistake, there'd be fewer mistakes in the world today. We can't usually test the system's function every second (but see *Unit Tests*, page 93, for a discussion of how hard we try). With acceptance tests, the sooner we catch the mistake, the sooner we can make the program work. The customer responsibility is to provide those acceptance tests as part of each iteration. If you can get them to the programmers by the middle of each iteration, the project will go faster. You will get more business value by the deadline. That's a promise.

There are many different ways to implement the acceptance testing on your project, and the programmers will pick one. We'll talk about that below. In any case, you need to specify the tests.

What must I test? you're probably asking. The official XP answer is, you only have to test the things that you want to have work. Let's be clear about that: if it's worth having the programmers build it, it's worth knowing that they got it right.

Some projects have a legacy system they are replacing, and they can get their test data from the legacy. In this case, your job will be to select the legacy inputs and outputs you want tested. Some projects use spreadsheets from the customer that provide the inputs and expected outputs. Smart XP programmers will extract the information from the spreadsheet automatically and read it into the system. Some projects use manually calculated values that are typed in by someone on the team.

Some customers give input numbers to the programmers and check the output by just reading it. There is an important issue with this one that has to be mentioned. This is an anti-pattern—a bad idea—called Guru Checks Output. Checking the output of a computer is very error-prone. It's easy to look at the numbers and decide that they look correct. It's also easy to be wrong when you do that. Far better to have the expected answers up front, even if they have to be computed by hand.

One more thing. The rights refer to repeatable tests. All tests in an XP project must be automated. We give you the ability to move very rapidly, and to change your requirements any time you need to. This means that the code will be changing rapidly. The only way to move rapidly with confidence is to have a strong network of tests, both unit and acceptance, that ensure that changes to the system don't break things that already work. The acceptance tests must be automated: insist on it as your right.

We aren't much into dire warnings and predictions, but here's one that's a sure thing: the defects in your system will occur where you don't test. Push your acceptance tests to the limit, in breadth and in depth. You'll be glad you did.

Automating the Tests

The tests must be automated, or you won't get your XP merit badges. However, there are lots of ways this can be done. The specific choice is up to your programmers. Here are some starting ideas:

- ✧ If the program is a batch program, reading inputs and producing outputs, make a standard series of input files, run the program, check the output manually (and carefully) once, and then write simple scripts that compare the test output to the known good output.
- ✧ Use the above trick for reports and lists from any program, batch or not.
- ✧ Build on the *xUnit* (page 105) testing framework. Write functional tests as programs. Better yet, make a little scripting language that the programmers can use. Then grow it and make it easier until the

customers can use it. Maybe provide a little GUI that displays more detail than the red bar/green bar.

✦ Allow the customers to set up tests in their favorite spreadsheet, then read in the test and execute it. Some teams read the spreadsheet data from exported files. Some actually use the "automation" feature of the spreadsheet to read the information. A few actually export test results back to the spreadsheet! This isn't as hard as it sounds—take a look at it and see if it's within your team's ability.

✦ Build an input recorder into the product, let the customers exercise it once to define a test. Spill output to files and check them automatically.

✦ Use simple file-based tools like grep and diff and Perl to check results. You can get a lot of testing automated very quickly with these tools.

Always build your acceptance tests to be automatic, but build the automation simply and incrementally as you actually need it. It's easy to get sucked into investing in test automation instead of business value. Get the tests automated, but don't go overboard.

Timeliness

Acceptance tests really need to be available in the same iteration as the story is scheduled. Think about it—you want to score the development based on getting stories done, and the only way to know if they are really done is to run the tests.

Programmers, you have the right to know what is needed. Insist on this right in the form of automated functional tests. You'll be glad you did.

Customers, you have the right to see progress in a running system, proven to work by automated tests that you specify. Insist on this right, and do your part by providing the necessary information.

Acceptance
Test Samples

At first it can be difficult figuring out how to do acceptance tests. With a little practice, it becomes easy.

Here are some of the sample stories from the story chapter, with suggestions for how they might be tested.

Union dues vary by union and are taken only in the first pay period of the month. The system computes the deduction automatically. The amount is shown in the attached table.

This is an easy one, of course: the test pays some employees from various unions and checks whether they are charged the right dues, in the first pay period. Another test checks the subsequent pay periods to make sure dues are not taken.

When a transaction causes a customer's account to go into overdraft, transfer money from the overdraft protection account, if any.

Also easy. Some sample customers, with and without overdraft protection. Test what happens if there isn't enough money in the overdraft account—note that the story is probably incomplete. If the customer writes the test correctly, the programmers will see and deal with the problem quickly enough.

When a transaction causes a customer's account to go into overdraft, send an e-mail showing the transaction and balance to the customer. If overdraft protection is in effect, show the overdraft transaction and the resulting account balances in the e-mail.

Same as previous test, except that e-mails should be sent. Send them all to a fixed account; have the programmers write code that reads them and checks their formats, so the test can be automatic.

Produce a statement for each account, showing transaction date, number, payee, and amount. A sample statement is attached—make the report look approximately like the sample.

It's tempting to look at the report manually. That way lies the dark side. Check the report once, very carefully, then compare it mechanically against the good one thereafter.

When the GPS has contact with two or fewer satellites for more than 60 seconds, it should display the message "Poor satellite contact," and wait for confirmation from the user. If contact improves before confirmation, clear the message automatically.

Functionally testing small hardware devices can be tricky. Do you have a version of the hardware hooked up to testing equipment that can read the display, provide fake satellite input, and so on? Depending on your cost of testing and need for reliability, this might be valuable enough to do.

Allow the user to add new service types to the system's initial list. For example, he may wish to add a special entry for getting the car washed at the high school's "free" wash. Include the standard fields amount and date, plus allow the user to add any additional text or numeric fields. Reports should automatically sum any numeric fields. (Programmer note: story needs splitting. Please separate text and numeric fields into two stories, plus one for the summing.)

This program, probably conceived as just an interactive GUI-based system, clearly needs a programmatic interface. It's not hard, given even a simple interface, to have a little scripting language set up that simulates GUI commands and checks report output. Remember to compare the report file to a correct one rather than check it by hand.

Chapter 6

Story Estimation

Customers need to know how much stories will cost in order to choose which ones to do and which to defer. Programmers evaluate stories to provide that information. Here's how.

If all stories were the same size, it would be easy to steer the project. We'd just do some of the most important stories and make note of how many we could do during an iteration. Then we'd just use that number to set our expectations for next time, and to select what to do by our preferred delivery date.

> *"Well, we're doing about five stories per week, and there are ten weeks till Comdex. We'll probably get about 50 done. Right now, it looks as if these are the ones we'll pick. To make sure we're always in the best possible shape, we'll do the most valuable ones first. Here are the best ten, let's do those over the next two weeks."*

After each iteration, we'd see how fast we were going, and adjust accordingly. And if our priorities changed and we brought in ten entirely different stories next time, that would be great. It would just make the product even better.

How fantastic this is! If we know how fast development is actually going, and how difficult the upcoming work is, we can have the best possible outcome our time and money can produce!

Well, all stories aren't usually quite the same size, but as the team goes along, you'll get better and better at knowing how big they are. Some may be worth one point, some may be worth two or three, some only one-half. If the team is doing ten points per week, it's just as easy to pick the most important ten points' worth as the most important ten stories. As the project progresses, estimates will get better and better, and your ability to steer will get better, too.

It's not easy to guess exactly how fast you will go at first, but it's easy to observe how fast you do go. Then, except for obvious adjustments like vacations and holidays, it's best to trust your actual speed and base your planning on how fast you're actually going.

Our mission here is to describe how to estimate stories. During the course of the project, it's best to do that comparatively. At the beginning, when you have no direct experience, there are some tricks you might want to use. We'll start with comparison.

During Project Flow, Estimate by Comparison

For an ongoing project, the work all takes on a kind of familiarity. Part of this is because one story is often just an elaboration of another closely related one. Plus, since you are keeping your objects clean and clear, you become more and more familiar with how to use them, and new requirements fall into place in familiar ways. During the flow of the project, take advantage of these facts.

Look at the story. What stories already implemented is it like? Does it access the database similarly to that one about the tax lookup? Does it produce a report similar to the one about parking tickets? Does it seem like a specialization of the purchasing business rules? As you think of stories that seem similar, wait for that Aha! moment when you think, "Why, it's just like…". That's the story to compare with.

There are a number of ways to handle the comparison once you have it. The most accurate would seem to be to record how long each story actually takes to implement, and then to estimate the new one the same way. But, it turns out, that doesn't work. The actual time to implement a story is made up of two components—how difficult the story is and how fast the team is going.

Back when you implemented the first story, perhaps support requirements were low and other projects weren't coming down. The programmers spent most of their time programming, and they got the story done in a week. But now, there are support requests coming in, new projects to plan, and lots of meetings going on. That same story, today, might take two weeks or more. Knowing that our new story is the same as one that took a week is good, but it isn't enough.

Here's what to do. We'll estimate story *difficulty*, using a simple point system. Local naming rules for these points apply. Some teams call them *perfect engineering weeks*, but other teams find this causes too much pressure trying to fit perfect weeks back into the real weeks that wind up being issued to us. Some projects call them Gummi Bears. No, really. You might prefer Story Estimation Units, or Bucks. Ron's favorite name, this week, is just to call them points.

You'll see in a bit that we recommend doing initial estimates by thinking in terms of time. Pass over that for now, and just accept that all the stories you have worked on are all classified, in points, somehow. Then, to estimate a new story, pick a completed one that is comparable. If it seems the same, give it the same number of points. If it seems twice as hard, give it twice as many. Half as hard, half. It's simple, and it's easy. The conversations go like this:

Jill says, "I think this is just like that one a couple of iterations ago, the historical report, where we had to connect to the database but also had to output those files."

Jack replies, "Yes, except this one has more files. I think this one is harder."

"You're right. Probably about 50 percent harder. How many points was the historical report?"

Jack, flipping through cards, finding the historical report, "It was a one pointer. Let's make this story one and a half."

It really becomes that simple. A quick discussion about what old story the new one is like, maybe a check of the old card to see how many points the old one was, and you've got an estimate. The team is doing many stories over many iterations and gets very good at this.

It's always best to estimate in pairs or groups—up to four works just fine—because having someone to talk with makes it easier and more accurate. The give and take helps a lot. We'll talk more about this in *Customer Defines Release* (page 55). Let's move on now to getting those initial estimates.

Early on, Start with Intuitive Time Estimates

You might want to express your estimates using a neutral term such as *points*, but the best way we know to start is with perfect engineering weeks. Here's how to do it.

Try to begin with a story that you can imagine how to do. If the story is so new to you that you can't imagine how to do it, then you need to do a *Spike Solution* (page 41). Basically a spike is just an experiment, where you do enough work to get a good feeling for how to implement the story.

If you do know approximately how to implement the story, chat with your team members, and try to get into coffee-room mode. You know, that frame of mind where you say, "I could implement that in a week if they'd just leave me alone to do it." That's your intuition at work, telling you how big the story is, without worrying about how much time you actually get just to program. That week, where you program perfectly all day every day, then go home and rest, and come in the next day fresh and ready to code—that's a perfect engineering week.

If you feel that you can do a story in one perfect week, give it one point. If you feel you can do it in two, give it two. If it feels like three, OK, give it three points, but consider asking the customer to *split the story* into two or more. And our advice is that if you start thinking you could do it in a month, your intuition has become too fuzzy. If your best estimate is four weeks or more, please have the customer split the story.

As soon as you have estimated the points for a few stories, start doing it both ways. Ask your intuition about its difficulty, get the points that way. Then compare the story to the others, asking yourselves which ones it's like in size. Check the points, and see if you get the same answer. For a new project, with fairly experienced programmers with reasonable intuition about the application, a team can go over 100 or more stories in a day or two, and rate them by difficulty.

It usually turns out that your initial ratings will be pretty accurate. But what's more important, as you remember from your rights (on page 7), you can change those assessments at any time. When you learn that something is easier or harder than you thought, you get to update the ratings on cards that are similar. The majority of times, you'll be rating stories as easier than you feared—after all, the whole team is learning, and for lots of stories, you'll even have built little tools. Sometimes, though, you may need to upgrade the story's difficulty. That's not a bad thing, because the truth is never a bad thing. Knowing the cost of things is how an XP team steers the project to success.

Spike Solution

It really is easy to estimate the difficulty of stories compared to other stories. Brainstorm what the tasks are a bit, then see what you've already done that is about that size, or twice the size, or half, or one and a half, as we described above.

But what if you haven't done anything like this story before? What if it's the beginning of the project and you haven't done anything at all?

The answer is simple: do some experimenting. We call such an experiment a *spike solution,* to remind us that the idea is just to drive through the entire problem in one blow, not to craft the perfect solution first time out. You need to know how long it will take to do something. To know that, you need to know how you'll go about it, but you don't really need to have done it all.

Here are some examples. None of these are made up—they are actual descriptions of spike solutions that people have used to learn how hard something was.

Balancing an Account

We are going to have accounts, like bank accounts, with transactions in them. We will need to compute the account balance.

This example was actually done live, by Ward Cunningham and Kent Beck, at an OOPSLA conference a few years ago. The first spike solution was to take a collection of numbers and add them up. Sounds dumb, doesn't it? But that's the essence of getting the account balance: take the numbers and add them up.

We mention this one first because it is so primal and simple. By doing this experiment you realize the fundamental simplicity of getting the account balance: just add 'em up. It pulls away all the separate issues of the Transaction class and the MonetaryAmount class and the ACID properties of the database, and lets us see balancing for what it is: get all the stuff and add it up.

Naturally the spike doesn't stop here. We might build a little Transaction object with an amount in it, make a vector of them, loop, and add them up. We might even make a little Monetary object, put it in the Transaction, make a vector, add them up. By this time, we're convinced: balancing an existing account will take less time to code than this description took to write up.

Formatted Reports

We are going to have a bunch of formatted reports. They will have different columns, and they all have to be totaled and subtotaled. Maybe we don't have a reporting tool—maybe we do. In either case, we need to estimate these reports. So we spike.

The spike? Make a collection of record objects—objects with data in them but no behavior. Give them a key field and a couple of values. Code the report, using whatever tools you have. First, just print them to get a feel for the shape of the loop. Print a total at the bottom. Then print a subtotal on each sequence break. This whole experience will probably take an hour or two. So the basics of reporting are easy.

Now look at formatting. Use your tools to format some numbers and dates in a few quaint and curious ways. See how hard it is to do.

Based on the report descriptions, number of fields and keys, and the hassle of formatting, estimate doing a report. Multiply by the number you have to do. (I'd assume the customer won't like any of the reports the first time and will change them an average of once each.)

If there are a lot of reports and the cost seems too high, do an experiment with a report generator or some table-driven thing, so you can see whether the customers can do their own reports. Keep it simple, no more than a day.

Database Access

While it runs, the system needs to access your SQL database to find the details for each item it processes. You want to know how long it will take to code this, and you also want to know how it will perform, in case you have to do something special.

You need a sample database to access. Anything will do. Write a simple SQL query that will return a few records. Test it in interactive mode. Code it into a program and send it across through your database connection. Note what goes wrong. Probably you won't get it across for a while, then probably you won't be able to deal with what comes back. Might take a day or so to get the first one working. If you've got experience and good DB connection software, it might just be an hour. After an hour or a day, you know what the code looks like to talk to the DB.

To get a sense of performance, take the above code and put it in a loop and time it. If you're in the ballpark, stop. If you're not, you'll have to do something special, like cache values. You've just identified the risk and put a number to it. There will be work to do, but you are already on the way to getting it caged.

What about the generated SQL? That could be tricky, couldn't it? Experiment with that separate from the connection. Generating the SQL is an exercise in string manipulation: we need to create a string that substitutes specific values into the various parts of the query. Maybe we need to make a list of the specific fields we want back. Maybe we need to put in one or more inquiry values. No big deal, just write code that formats that string and checks it. Think of it as coding most of the SQL by hand, then just plugging in the variable bits.

Automatic E-Mail

The system has to e-mail the support people when certain things happen, so as to beep their beepers. How hard will this be? No biggie to detect the error or format the message. We can estimate that. But it could be awful to send the e-mail; we've never done that.

I just surfed the Web, looking for "e-mail protocol." Item 22 on my list is a Java applet that tells me about the SMTP protocol and lets me type in example lines. Looks like it is all done with text messages. Should be easy.

Write a little program to connect to the e-mail API on your machine, and send a simple e-mail to yourself. It probably won't work. Debug it. After an hour or so, or a day or so, you'll get it to work. Now you have the sketch of the code for doing e-mail, and you can estimate the story.

Spiking for Estimation

Remember the essence of the spike: you don't know enough about solving some problem to be able to estimate it. Therefore, write some sample code, so that you'll learn enough to make an estimate.

In this case, you are not here to drain the swamp; you're just here to kill one alligator. As soon as that gator is dead, and you can estimate how long the solution will take, move on.

Estimation Summary

We programmers estimate stories in points, based on perfect engineering time, and we keep track of how many points we can do in each iteration. That lets our customer steer us to success by choosing the best combination of stories given the time and money available.

Except at the beginning, most stories are best estimated by comparing them with other stories already completed, and giving them points according to their relative size. It turns out, as you'll find, that programmers are generally very good at making this comparison. Sometimes, at any stage in the project, stories will come along that you're not ready to compare. In this case you do a spike solution, a quick experiment that prepares you to estimate.

Even the strangest stories will yield to a little creative brainstorming. For some whimsical evidence of this, check the bonus track *How to Estimate Anything* on page 185.

At the beginning of the project, use your group intuition to get that "I could do that in a week" feeling, then set the initial points based on that intuition. We recommend giving the points a neutral term, rather than *weeks*, just because it keeps the tension down a bit as you track your implementation velocity. As soon as you begin to get experience with the relative difficulty of the stories, you can, and should, update the points for the remaining ones. This gives the customer the best opportunity to steer you to success.

Interlude

Sense of Completion

XP's nested planning and programming cycles keep the project on track and provide a healthy sense of accomplishment at frequent intervals.

Most projects go on for months; some go on for years. To keep from going mad with the never-ending pounding out of code—even beautiful, well-crafted code—every project needs punctuation. The best punctuation a programmer can get is a sense of completion. XP's planning cycles provide a rhythm of cycles within cycles, each with its own moment of completion.

Running the tests successfully gives the programmer a sense of completion every few minutes. Share this small joy with your partner.

Finishing a task provides a sense of completion every few hours. Share with the other programmers, take a break, or maybe switch partners.

Completing a story is an important milestone. Each one provides a sense of completion. Share with customers and programmers or have a small ritual. (Ann favors an end-zone dance.)

Wrapping up an iteration completes several stories and opens the door for the next accomplishments. Share with the whole team. Consider bringing in pizza or some other little celebration.

Each release provides a major sense of completion. New business value is in the hands of the customer. This is a good day! Break out the champagne!

These are important moments. They punctuate the work and give it a sense of meaning and progress. Without these moments, the work becomes drudgery, a never-ending death march.

Programmers Set the Rhythm

Programmers, every day you are responsible for creating your own sense of completion. Work on one story at a time. Work on one task from that story's tasks. Write a test that you need for that task. Run it just in case it already works. Code till it does work, running the tests frequently. When the test you're working on runs, take a moment. Tick it off in your mind—one more little bit of completion.

Write the tests one at a time, and test and code on the task until all the necessary tests run. Take a moment. Task done! Let yourself feel that little triumph. Cross the task off your list. Give it a little flourish. Task done!

Is the code in good shape for release—not necessarily finished, but able to run all the tests? Maybe it's a good time to run the tests and release some code. Code released! Life is good.

Work on one story at a time. When all the tests for that whole story run, take a moment. A whole story is done! That's very good. The customer will get that card back marked complete. Life is very good.

When a story is done, it's definitely time to run all the tests and release your code.

Have a little ritual that goes with code release. Maybe get one of those little bells that you whack on the top when you want service at the counter. Give it one whack whenever you successfully release. When someone else gives the bell a whack, give them a little appreciation—soft applause, quiet cheers of "Yeah."

Punctuate the project. Enjoy those moments of completion.

At the end of the iteration, make a little production of handing the completed stories back to the customer. "These are done." Give yourselves a little applause—this is good! If some stories aren't finished, so be it. Consider announcing those first, so you can close the iteration on an up note. "These stories didn't get done, explain explain." Pause. "Here," handing over the stack, "are the stories we completed." Take a moment, congratulate yourselves.

Customers, you should feel this moment as well. Some of what you asked for is complete. A bite has been taken out of your problem. Enough bites and you'll have something of value, something you can use.

Celebrate the moment. Programmers are like puppies, only not as mature. We need constant encouragement to keep going. So tell us: "Good programmers, good. Nice programmers." Maybe toss us a bone or a Programmer Treat like a package of red licorice.

Your project is going to go on for a long time. Sometimes it may seem even longer. Work is fun and enjoyable when there's a feeling of accomplishment, a sense of completion. Provide those moments, and bask in them. Succeed every day, and make sure that everyone knows you are succeeding every day.

Chapter 7

Small Releases

The outermost XP cycle is the release. Small and frequent releases provide early benefit to the customer while providing early feedback to the programmers. Here are some thoughts on how to make it happen.

If your customer knows now just exactly what she wants, and if by the time you're done she's still going to want the same thing, it may be the first time in software history that this has happened. Probably there will be a prize for you somewhere. It's much more likely that as you steer the project, you'll be changing direction, a little or a lot. As you find out what's easy to do and what's more costly, you'll be making better and better decisions about what to do and when to do it.

One of the most important things you can do on an XP project is to release early and release often. If possible, wait no more than two months to release a version of the software, and release every couple of months thereafter. And we don't mean a demo version; we mean an actual version that does something useful. Even though you don't *really* have to release for six months or a year, releasing every couple of months can really pay off. You don't want to pass up the chance to learn what users really want. You don't want to pass up the increasing confidence that will come from showing people that you have done something useful. And you don't want to pass up the sheer thrill of releasing useful software into the universe.

Even though you'd like to, we know that small releases are impossible in your situation. We accept that you just couldn't do it. But just imagine for a moment that you could actually get some useful subset of the software into the customers' hands. Not something they'd demo and comment on and set aside, but something they'd use every day. They would learn a lot about what they really wanted, and you'd be that much more capable of steering the project to success.

Even better, if the releases are actually useful, you're delivering real business value to the customers, which will keep them happy and keep them coming back. It will build confidence and keep them supporting the effort, even if once in a while things get rough.

OK, you're convinced that it would be nice, but it just couldn't happen with your product. Your product is all-or-nothing; it just couldn't really be useful except when it's really pretty done. Well, believe us, it's worth thinking about it. Of all the projects we've been involved with that failed, almost all of them would have been successful had they delivered a little functionality over time, instead of waiting and waiting and waiting. So let's take some examples of projects that couldn't possibly deliver something early, and try to think of things we could deliver early after all. You probably won't be so lucky that we'll pick yours and solve it—fact is, you know more about your project than we do—but practicing on ours may help you find your own small releases.

Payroll Is All or Nothing

Clearly, you can't release a payroll program incrementally. If it doesn't compute the paycheck correctly, it's of no use at all. What good would it be to have a payroll program that could get your pay right but couldn't compute your taxes or take out your health insurance costs?

Well, setting aside the obvious value of a payroll that didn't take out your taxes, let's think about this a bit.

If there's already a legacy payroll program in place, maybe you could replace the hours times rate part of it with the new one, allowing you to stop using one of the old COBOL programs and get some good out of the new improved calculations.

What about all those adjustment cards that have to be keypunched from forms filled out by the payroll clerks? You're going to have a new GUI to put those adjustments right into the system. How about doing that GUI first, and instead of putting data into the system (which doesn't exist yet), write them out to a file and feed them into the payroll. You could save the keypunching expense, probably improve reliability, and allow adjustments to be done further into the week because you would not have to wait for the keypunchers. The clerks could offer better service with the standalone GUI.

Is there some complex calculation that the old payroll can't do quite right, or that needs updating soon? How about replacing that part of the legacy program with transactions generated by a little chunk of the new program. The new program has to have that part written anyway, and now you can save the cost of updating the legacy program.

Or how about diverting employees from the legacy stream who are capable of being paid by the new program and paying them there? The new program would get exercised, and at least those individuals would get the benefit of being in the new system. If, a few pay cycles down, more features let you divert more people in, great. And if someone's pay situation gets too complex for the evolving new program, just divert them back to the legacy.

Now each of these schemes has a little extra cost associated with it, in order to bring it on line. But the benefits would be immense in the delivery of improved value, the feeling of accomplishment, the better feedback, and the better focus of the whole team on delivering value.

Personnel System

You're replacing your personnel system with a new one. Obviously you need an integrated database and can't release the system until it does everything the old one does, plus all the new things you've thought of. There's just no way you can release this incrementally.

This could turn into one of those horrible tail-chasing exercises where there's always just one more feature that you have to put into the new system before it's ready. Just don't go there.

Instead, what if we made our database compatible with the old one, but with new relational tables for new features that are needed, and delivered some of those new features. We could produce new reports that summarized the use of the new features, and we could produce new versions of some of the old reports to show combined values.

Maybe we could do the GUI trick like from the payroll example, where we gave the users a better way to input certain transactions. Maybe we could even put up a little Web interface and let employees enter their own address changes and telephone numbers.

Tax Package

Here's one we wish we had thought of a few years ago. A professional tax package isn't useful unless it does some minimum number of forms, and the minimum is very large. So building a new Windows-based professional tax package is a multiyear investment. And there's just no way to release just part of it.

Well, if your company already has a DOS-based package that's comprehensive, how about putting a Windows GUI on top of it, and using that calculation expertise until you get the more powerful object-oriented incremental calculation engine working?

How about using individual forms calculations from the DOS program and replacing them incrementally with the new engine?

How about using the existing forms print capability of the DOS version, together with its non-WYSIWYG output display, until the screens that look just like tax forms are done?

Distributed Manufacturing Control System

You are building a new microcomputer-based distributed factory control system. There will be these cool little micros at each station, all networked together, cooperating to control the entire factory. You need control modules and control programs for all the machines that might be there in the factory. And you need a very sophisticated distributed object system to make sure it all works. There's just no way you can release anything early.

Well, how about releasing a single module that controls some specific machine, and that plugs into the legacy system, emulating an old-fashioned controller. Surely your micro-based system could raise and lower a few electrical levels to make it look like the old modules and even respond to centralized signals telling it what to do.

Then do another kind of module and another. Choose them so they are likely to want to talk to each other. When a factory needs a couple of these, let's hook just those modules together in a distributed fashion, letting the rest of the place run on centralized control.

It might be a bit tricky, and it would be wasteful in that when the last distributed module went in, all that centralized control code would be unnecessary. But in the years between the ability to release one little controller, and the release of the last bit of the fully distributed system, you could make so much money and learn so much!

Air Traffic Control System

Planes get handed off between control areas, and in times of emergency certain areas take over wider areas of control. So all these systems have to talk to each other, and replacing the nation's outmoded control system with a new one is an immense task.

OK, we admit it, we don't know anything about air traffic control. But we do know that a current theory is that the planes should control themselves, communicating with each other and adjusting their paths the way that birds do, maintaining certain preferred distances, increasing their desire to move away when they get too close, and so on. One of the problems with this system is that not all planes would be smart enough to do this. In addition, what would happen if a plane lost its ability to sense and be sensed by the others?

Would it be possible to dedicate certain altitudes and flight paths to the new planes? Would it be possible to have on-ground control computers watching for planes that couldn't communicate, and either controlling them from the ground or handing them back to the existing legacy ATC?

Summary

We hope you're getting the idea. Inside almost every large program there are lots of little programs trying to get out. You might have to do a little extra work around the edges to get these pieces useful on their own, but it can be well worth your while. You'll learn lots more, and you will actually be *delivering value*. Would that be cool, or what?

Therefore, put all your thoughts behind this simple idea: release little bits, to be used by real customers, very frequently. It will enable you to deliver the most value in the shortest time, with great confidence and low stress. We also think it will grow new hair on your head and help you lose weight, but we're not sure about those two. The rest—we're sure.

Chapter 8

Customer Defines Release

In each release cycle, the customer controls scope, deciding what to do and what to defer, to provide the best possible release by the due date. Work fits into the calendar based on business value, difficulty, and the team's implementation velocity.

As the XP customer, you have a right to an overall plan, to know what can be accomplished, when, and at what cost. You have the right to change your mind, to substitute functionality, and to change priorities. Not surprisingly, you also have corresponding responsibilities. The most important of those responsibilities is to define software releases and to manage scope to get a quality release out on time. It's best to plan a series of *Small Releases* (page 49), but small or large, the releases are up to you.

In XP, releases are made up of iterations, where each iteration implements stories, which are made up of tasks. Both releases and iterations have three phases: exploration, commitment, and steering. Releases, iterations, and the phases make up the XP planning process, and they are the subject of the next few chapters.

During the exploration phase of planning a release, you'll be writing stories, defining what the system needs to do. You'll be thinking about the business value of each story—is it essential, highly valuable, or just a good idea. Your chief weapon is business value.

In that same exploration phase, the programmers will be experimenting with ways of building the system, trying experiments that inform them how costly the various stories and features will be.

Most teams remember to do the exploration part of writing the stories since it's hard to proceed without them. But don't forget the programming part of exploration—take a week or so to experiment with the application before trying to proceed to commitment.

The exploration activities culminate in the commitment phase of planning the release. It goes like this, and the tune is our own invention:

You'll hand your story cards over to the programmers for estimation. Then you sit back, listen, and wait for questions. If the programmers want to know whether you want a Windows-specific GUI or one that is Web-based, you'll answer them. (Sometimes you'll have to get them to explain their question first. That's OK; keep after them until they do.)

The programmers are trying to estimate the difficulty of each story card you have given them. They're doing that so that you can decide, based on business value and implementation cost, what should be in the next release.

Sometimes the programmers will find one of your stories too hard to estimate. That doesn't mean you can't have it; it just means that it's got too much in it for them to make a valid single estimate. This is important to you: You want the estimates to be as good as possible, so that your selection of what to do and what to defer will be as good as possible.

Sometimes you just have to explain what you meant in the story. When this happens, consider ripping that story up and writing a new one. It feels good and shows the programmers how flexible you are.

Sometimes the story is just too big. In XP, the programmers aren't allowed to estimate things in months of effort. We've learned that those estimates are too often wild guesses. So even if the programmers are pretty sure about a big story, we don't let them estimate it that way. Instead, they'll ask you to split a story. Often this will be obvious and easy. You asked for a lot of things in one story. Just split the things out, tearing up the old card (feels good, doesn't it?) and writing new ones. If, while you're at it, you can keep things of like priority together, that will help later. An easy way to do that is to choose the most important thing, write it on a card, then the next, and so on. Don't worry about getting too many cards. Too few is a problem, but if there are too many, you can just clip them together.

Listen to the programmers as they estimate your stories. They'll be talking about technical things, but you'll usually get the drift of what they intend. That will tell you, in turn, whether they are understanding what you want. You may hear, from time to time, things that make you think maybe they don't understand the story. If that happens, stop them and inquire. If they've got it right, fine, but if not, give them the straight story and let them carry on. You might want to tear up the card and improve it, of course. Feel the power of change? Wonderful, isn't it?

After a while (and the first time around it could be a long time), the programmers will have assigned a cost number to each story. Different teams call this number different things: difficulty points, perfect engineering weeks, Bucks, or even Gummi Bears. Whatever the name, these numbers are the same thing: estimates of how difficult each story is to build. With just one more fact, you're ready to choose the stories for the release plan.

To know what to schedule for the first release, you need to know how fast the team can implement stories.

What? you may be asking. I need all these things done by the release date. I want it all. Well, as the song goes, you can't always get what you want, but if you try, you can get what you need. Here's how you do that.

The programmers will tell you how many points they can do in a given period of time. We call that number Project Velocity. If they're estimating with perfect weeks as the basis, they'll probably do one point per programmer, every two or three calendar weeks. If they're estimating in perfect days, they'll probably do one to three points per programmer per week. (Don't get excited. Those guys aren't going faster, they're just measuring feet per minute instead of miles per hour.)

At the beginning of the first project of this kind for the team, this number will be a guess. But as soon as you get experience doing the stories, the team will measure the actual velocity. You can use that experience-based number to steer the release. And that's your job.

Once the stories are all estimated, you have a bunch of story cards back in your hands, with business value that you understand and difficulty points of one, two, or three. Sometimes one and a half, but don't worry, someone in the room probably has a calculator. The velocity is, say, five points per two-week iteration.

You know how many iterations there are between now and the scheduled release date. Suppose there are six. Then you should plan to get about 30 points done by then, or five times six. Go through your cards and pick the ones with the highest business value adding up to no more than 30 points. That's your plan.

Sounds easy, doesn't it? Well, it is easy, except for one thing. You may well wish you could have 35 points instead of 30. In fact, you surely will wish that, since all things being equal, more features are generally better than fewer.

Our advice is to go with the numbers. If the numbers say you can do five points per week, and you could get your 35 total points if the team could just do six, resist your temptation to plan for six. Work on getting the team's velocity up. But plan based on your actual speed, not your hopes. That keeps your plan closer to reality and keeps you focused on your most important role, which is steering the project to success.

The team will go faster if it's winning than if it's falling short. Give team members a chance to exceed their goals—they may surprise you. And your own experience of the project will improve as you learn to guide it to success.

As the customer, you define the release by selecting the best combination of stories that the team's performance suggests can be accomplished. As you learn more about performance and more about how the system is shaping up, you'll adjust and tune the combination of stories you request. An XP team will always adjust immediately and work on just the things you need to make the system as good as it can be within your time and budget.

Release Planning Meeting

In its simplest form, the steps to a release plan are:

1. Write enough stories to define a successful product.
2. Do any necessary exploration.
3. Estimate the difficulty of implementing each story.
4. Estimate the speed of story implementation.
5. Choose stories for the first release based on business value and difficulty.

The purpose of the release plan is to prime XP's continuous planning circle of life. No plan can predict the future perfectly, but planning can help you steer the project to success. Think of it this way:

If you knew how long it would take to build each desired feature in your product, you could do a really good job of picking the best mix of features given your time and budget.

No one can tell you exactly, far in advance, just how long it will take to build software. We're just the only folks who admit it. What we can do, instead, is to teach your programmers how to estimate the difficulty of each feature, and how to measure the speed of implementing features.

If you know how hard it is to build each piece of what you have in mind, and you know how fast you can build things, you can accurately estimate what you can have done by your due date—or when you will have any batch of features done.

In *Story Estimation* (page 37), we describe how you get a story estimate. Here's how you use them.

The customer brings to the meeting all the stories she would like to have for the first release. The programmers divide up into small groups, take batches of the cards, and pencil onto each card their estimate of its difficulty. If they have questions about the story, they ask and the customer answers. The programmers quickly discuss the tasks they'll have to do for the story, and they record the estimate.

All the groups look at all the stories. The rule we use is that if a second group thinks the story is easier, they'll check with the first group and ask how they got their answer. If they still think it's easier, they can reduce the number on the card. Formally, we only let folks reduce estimates, but of course if the discussion identifies something forgotten, the programmers can increase the difficulty rating.

Rate the easiest stories as one point. Rate the others as twos, threes, and so on.

Soon (as you improve at this, you can do over a hundred stories in a morning) all the stories will have a difficulty estimate.

You give the stories back to the customer and tell her what the anticipated velocity will be. This is a simple number: "We estimate that the team will do ten points in each iteration."

Based on that estimate, and the due date, and the customer's knowledge of the value of each story, she can select the ones that will make for the best release by the date. That selection of stories makes up the release plan.

Some teams find it interesting and comforting to lay the cards out against the calendar; in the first iteration, we'll probably do these ten points, in the second those, and so on. Experienced teams don't even bother, because they know that the priorities will change and that they're completely comfortable working on whatever the customer comes up with.

Either way, the main thing to remember is this: this is a plan, an estimate, and not a fact. What will happen isn't just what you laid out here. It'll be a lot like that, but it'll be somewhat better or somewhat worse for most projects. Once in a while you'll get really lucky and do lots better, and sometimes you might not come close.

However it goes, the good news is that you don't have to wait till the end. Remember that in the iteration plan, every couple of weeks you have a chance to reassess where you are and how fast you are going. So you will have every opportunity to steer your project to success.

Chapter 9

Iteration Planning

Inside each release, an Extreme team plans just a few weeks at a time with clear objectives and solid estimates.

As the XP customer, you have the right to get the highest possible value out of every programming week. XP projects work in short "iterations" of two or three weeks, and you select the work to be done in each of those iterations. Your mission is to select work that will maximize the business value completed by the end of the iteration.

Supporting your customer rights, the programmers agree to work on the stories that you define, in the order you request. For you to do the best job of steering the project, you and the programmers need to plan the work in short chunks, which we call iterations, with tighter estimates of the work effort than were provided for release planning. The process goes like this:

During release planning, discussed in *Customer Defines Release* (page 55), you considered the business value of each story, while the programmers assigned difficulty points to each story, and they told you their estimated velocity, also in points. Perhaps your team has a velocity of 30 points per iteration. To prepare for the iteration planning meeting, select from all your stories, your favorites, up to a total of 30 points. Pick out a few extras, just in case. Many customers bring all their story cards to the meeting, with the ones for this iteration on top of the stack.

Your role in the meeting is to present and describe the stories one at a time, and the programmers will quickly define programming tasks for each story. When all the stories have been presented and tasked, the programmers will sign up for work and estimate the tasks. If there's too little or too much to do based on the stories you bring in, you get to decide which ones to add or remove.

During iteration planning, therefore, the conversation swings back and forth. You explain a story, with the programmers asking questions. As they begin to understand the story, the programmers brainstorm the tasks for it and put them on the board. Then you go to the next story.

When all the stories have been explained and tasked, there is a brief flurry of activity while the programmers sign up and estimate the work. Usually at the end there is some balancing to be done. Programmers with too much to do trade with those who don't have enough. And often you will need to help out by removing some less important work from the board. Occasionally, you'll even get to add more. In all cases, it's most effective to do the adjustment rather than try to cram just a little more in. It is tempting to push the programmers to try a little harder, and usually they'll give in at the slightest push. But in the end, their actual velocity, not their good wishes, are your best friend in steering to success.

If you are planning to meet someone for dinner, in front of their hotel, and it will take you half an hour to get there, it won't help to tell him it'll be 15 minutes. He'll just have 15 anxious minutes of waiting. It's better to plan your dinners, and your projects, based on your best measurements of actual performance.

The team won't lay back. When they get things done early—and often they will—they'll ask you for more to do. When that's the way you work, everyone gets to feel good. And folks who feel good work together better.

The Planning Meeting

There are three critical steps to iteration planning:

1. The customer presents user stories.
2. The team brainstorms engineering tasks.
3. The programmer signs up for and estimates the work.

Customer Presents User Stories

The customer presents the user stories to ensure that the team understands what is to be done. The most effective way to understand a requirement is to discuss it.

This begins the exploration phase of the iteration plan: explaining and understanding the stories to be done. The customer has selected the stories to be implemented during this iteration. She reads each story card, and the team members ask any questions they have until they understand the story. Each team member is responsible for having a good grasp of what the story requires.

Team Brainstorms Engineering Tasks

The team brainstorms the engineering tasks to build a common picture of the system design, down to the detail necessary to implement the stories. This step often allows the customer to see places where the programmers don't understand the story after all. Observing the design process builds common knowledge and confidence throughout the team.

Exploration continues as you and the programmers break the stories down into tasks. After a story is understood, the programmers brainstorm the tasks necessary to implement the story. Each team member is responsible for contributing as much as possible and for getting a good understanding of what will be done to implement the story.

Often the approach will be clear to all, as the story will be a simple extension of existing features. Other times there will be two or more possible approaches. Of these the team picks the simplest that could possibly work. Sometimes no solution presents itself immediately. In this case, the team will decide to work on an experiment (*Spike Solution*, page 41) for the story. The best thing to do is to time-box the experiment to a day or two. You're trying to learn how to solve the problem; you're not actually solving it.

Programmer Signs Up for Work and Estimates

Programmers sign up for work to allow individuals or pairs to accept the primary responsibility for completing specific work. The team does not force assignments on anyone, although someone signing up may ask for help from anyone and will receive it.

Programmers estimate their own work to provide the most accurate possible prediction of what will be accomplished. In addition, programmers feel more commitment to work that is scheduled for completion in a time they can believe in.

Now we begin the commitment phase, signing up for work and estimating it. After all the stories and tasks are presented, programmers sign up for the work to be done. It's possible to sign up for all the tasks for a given story or just for specific tasks. Each programmer signs up for as much work as she believes she can accomplish during the iteration, making estimates and keeping track as she goes along.

It is usually best to estimate at the task level, even if you are signing up for the whole story. If you're not clear on what a story or task entails, ask other members of the team. You might even ask how long similar things have taken, but try hard to use your own estimates and not to be swayed by the opinions of the other programmers.

Sign Up for Stories

It's certainly legal for programmers to mix and match tasks among stories. However, we think it's preferable, wherever practical, that you sign up for all the tasks on a story, rather than picking and choosing. The reason is that it'll help ensure that stories get fully completed.

Suppose that story A has ten points' worth of tasks in it, and I sign up for seven of them and you sign up for three. Well, you might work on other important tasks, especially if they add up to a story, and put off doing the three. That could put story A in jeopardy. How would the team notice this problem?

You could have programmers accept responsibility to watch stories, even if they don't sign up for all the tasks. Then the programmer who owns the story might wander over and coordinate getting the three, but not all programmers are assertive enough to do this. Instead, they'll wait, or work on something less important, rather than get their story out.

You might get lucky. Someone else might notice the three tasks not getting checked off the board and raise the issue, but if no one is "on the hook" for the story, outstanding tasks may not get noticed.

If no one feels responsibility for the story, then only the tracker is likely to notice problems. (See *Tracking,* page 152.) This puts a complex burden on the tracker to notice and will cause tasks to be reallocated. This isn't a good thing. Far better to have a single programmer take responsibility for each story. The simplest way to do that is for individual programmers to sign up for whole stories where possible, or to have an individual take responsibility for the whole story even if she hasn't signed up for all the tasks. That's what we recommend.

If there are tasks on the story that you just can't do, then pair with the person who can do them. That way you'll learn something and you'll see to it that your story gets done. If it's physically impossible for you two to work together, you have to fall back on far less effective approaches, like following up, nagging, and begging.

One more point on signing up for stories. What if the task of brainstorming done by the team isn't sufficient to complete the story? What if no one remembered that you have to create an input record format? Well, we hope someone will notice, but if there's no one on the hook for the whole story, chances are too good that no one will notice.

Notice also the connection to collective ownership. (See *Programming,* page 71.). Normally, if you need something done, you and your partner just do it. When there's an artificial division between the things you can and can't do, the whole process slows down. Wherever possible, avoid having specialists. They'll just become bottlenecks. Turn them into partners and expert helpers instead.

An Iteration Planning Practice

Here's one way to do iteration planning. It isn't the only one, but it has been used many times and works well. Perhaps you should try it until you work out a scheme of your own.

The team gathers around a whiteboard for the iteration plan. It often helps if someone acts as facilitator or director to keep things on track.

The customer stands at the whiteboard, writes the name of one story on the board, and describes what the story means. The team asks questions and the group discusses the story, until they're sure they get it, but no longer.

Then the team proceeds to brainstorm the tasks for that story, while it is fresh in mind, writing short names for the tasks on the whiteboard right under the story name. It might look like this:

> *Process Union Dues Refunds*
> >   *Create format for transaction*
> >   *Add transaction to accepted transactions list*
> >   *Create Union Dues Refund Station*

Then the customer puts another story on the board, and the process continues until enough stories are on the board.

Now it's time to sign up. Programmers who are particularly interested in some area jump up and put their initials on the board beside the things they want to do. In more civilized environments, you might ask for volunteers, but it's more fun to scramble. Other programmers who don't care what they work on in this iteration will hang back and pick up whatever is left over. If you're a newer member, it's usually a good idea to sign up early, so you can balance your need to learn with what you already know.

It is always appropriate to ask another programmer to help you if you sign up for some particular thing. That programmer will always answer yes—it's a rule.

As programmers sign up, they estimate each thing they sign up for. They stop signing up when their estimates reach their capacity for this iteration.

If there is too much on the board, the customer decides what to take off, and adjustments are made to sign-ups. If there is too little, the customer adds more stories as at the beginning. Continue until the board is just right.

At this point, all the stories and tasks on the board are signed up for and estimated. Our original story and tasks might look like this, with Chet signed up:

Process Union Dues Refunds
chet	*1.0*	*Create format for transaction*
chet	*0.5*	*Add transaction to accepted transactions list*
chet	*1.0*	*Create Union Dues Refund Station*

Note that it isn't necessary that a single programmer sign up for all the tasks on a story, and sometimes there's a good reason not to. In general, though, it's nice to have a single person responsible for making sure the story gets done.

You may find another way of doing iteration planning that's better than this one. If you do, please let us know. Just remember the three key parts: Customer presents stories, team brainstorms tasks, and programmers sign up and estimate.

Chapter 10

Quick Design Session

*Within each iteration, programmers don't stand alone. Here's a
technique to help programmers move forward with courage.
Make it part of your team's ritual.*

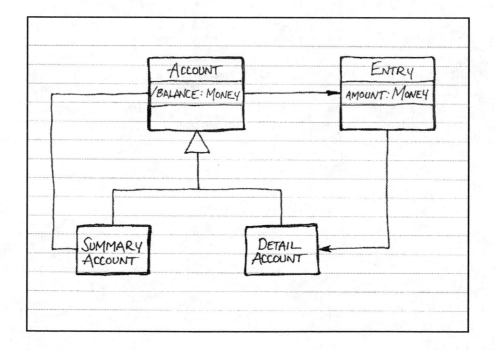

Truth is, once you have broken down a story into tasks, you often already really know how to implement it. Often the best thing to do is just to proceed to "Test-first programming." But if you aren't clear on just what to do, or if you would like a little reassurance, or if you would like a few additional ideas, have a quick design session.

Get a few people together and spend a few minutes sketching out the design. Ten minutes is ideal—half an hour should be the most time you spend to do this.

Do a CRC design with a few cards, or sketch some UML on the whiteboard or a sheet of paper. The idea is to understand the objects involved in what we're about to do, and to understand how to implement them, or change them, to accomplish the task.

It's important not to spend much time at this, because we'll do the most learning in the first few minutes. After that, the best thing to do is to let the code participate in the design session—move to the machine and start typing in code. Proceed test-first if you can. Otherwise perhaps work in a workspace or write some simple objects to get the feel of the solution. Listen to what the code tells you about what it wants to be. Then go for the real thing.

The purpose of such a design session is to eliminate our fear that we might not know what to do. Truth is, we probably do know what to do, though we'll certainly get some good ideas from our colleagues in the session. Listen to those ideas, absorb them, and then get to it.

Don't waste time arguing over different alternatives. Hear each alternative, embrace each idea, and make sure you understand it. Then pick the simplest one that could possibly work, every time. If a couple of ideas seem plausible, try them both for a few minutes, pick the simplest one that could possibly work, and get to it.

Chapter 11

Programming

It's called Extreme Programming, after all. Here's how we do the programming part of things.

In the iteration plan, the team received stories from the customer, broke them down into tasks, and signed up to do them. Here's how that "doing" gets done.

An XP programmer works with a partner. All production code is written by two people, sitting together at one machine. We call that *Pair Programming* (page 87). Your partners will vary over time: most XP teams switch partners many times per day. But for some tasks, you will probably work with just one primary partner, switching only to address some particular problem or when your partner is away. And, of course, sometimes you'll be helping someone else with their task.

The pair work on just one task at a time. Programming is hard enough without trying to do more than one thing at a time. After completing each task, the pair will integrate it into the software already released, then run all the unit tests in the entire system, making sure that they all run at 100 percent. Then they'll release the tests and code for their task into the repository. Tasks are released one at a time because the project goes best when everyone is working on the most current code all the time. The best way to do that is to integrate often. We call that *Continuous Integration* (page 78).

As the pair work, they'll proceed by writing tests first, then "fixing" them to work. Test a little, code a little. There's a long example of this in *Test First, by Intention* on page 107. The basic idea is that we always test whether the feature works, even when we know it doesn't, and then we make it work. This process has two great benefits. First of all, it makes us focus on *using* the feature before we build it. Since we'll build it once and use it frequently, writing the test first makes us concentrate on the interface design issue, not the algorithm. Testing first gives us better design.

Testing first also gives us tests. Tests—called unit tests when written by the programmers for the programmers—are what let us go fast and fearlessly. Every feature that XP programmers build must have *Unit Tests* (page 93), and those tests must test *Everything That Could Possibly Break* (page 233). And every time we release any software, each and every one of those unit tests must be run and must score 100 percent.

As the pair works, they will write new classes, but of course they will also be using existing classes. Often they'll find that they need to add features to those classes in support of their task. When this happens, the pair makes the necessary changes. We call this process *Collective Code Ownership* (page 75). It just means that everyone owns every class, so that anyone is authorized to improve it at any time. But wait, you're asking, why doesn't that lead to chaos and unreliability, as people who don't know my class work on it? Well, read that section to find out. Here's a hint: think about how pair programming, unit tests at 100 percent, and continuous integration might work together.

As we code, we try hard to express our *intention* first, then the algorithm. That idea, too, is demonstrated in *Test First, by Intention* on page 107, so be sure to check it out. The basic idea is this: when we learned to program, we learned by solving specific problems, like *go through all the personnel and compute the total of their salaries*. So we thought immediately about the algorithm and ended up with something like this:

```
totsal = 0.0;
for ( i = 0; i < nPers; i++) {
      pers = persons[i].
      sal = pers.salary();
      totsal += sal }
return totsal;
```

Now, when you run across that chunk of code a few weeks later, it takes only a few moments to figure out what it is, namely, compute total salary. And if it's expressed this way, it's not much harder or much easier:

```
totsal = 0.0;
for ( i = 0; i < nPers; i++) {
      totsal += persons[i].salary() }
return totsal;
```

Programming by expressing intention just means that the code would somehow express the idea of getting the total salary. Most likely in this case, we'd make it a class method on the *Person* class and name it something clever like *totalSalary*. Why do we do this? Our chief reason is clarity. Clarity and speed. Our two chief reasons are clarity and speed. Clarity, speed, and reduced documentation. Our three chief reasons . . .

Expressing intention makes the code clear the next time we, or other programmers, pass by. Since we share the code ownership, the next person passing through may well be new to the area. If the code says things like "*totalSalary*," the programmer will get it more quickly and will be able to change it more reliably. He'll more readily notice that the code exists and will, therefore, reuse existing code instead of accidentally duplicating the loop that he didn't notice buried somewhere else strange. If the meaning of the method is clear, we don't need to write a comment or a document about it, and if the method is where it should be (e.g., on the *Person* class), we won't have to draw road maps and train everyone. Want a method about persons? Look on the *Person*. This makes everything go more smoothly and quickly. It's a good thing.

Working in pairs as we do and sharing ownership of all the code, it's a good idea if we all program the same way. We need to name things similarly, so we'll all know where to look. We need to format things similarly, so we'll all see code that looks like what we expect. We need to create objects in standard ways, and so on. So every XP team needs to have a *Coding Standard* (page 79). The team needs to agree on it, so don't worry too much. Having everything look the same helps everyone go fast, so be reasonable about your favorite curly bracket style when it comes time to decide. You'll quickly adapt to the new standard, so no stress, OK?

As we code, we always try to use *Simple Design* (page 75). We do this in two key ways. First, when we are thinking about how to do something (having already expressed our *intention* to do it), we think about, and generally do, the simplest thing that could possibly work. Will an array do? Use an array. Will an if statement do? Use one. Will a case statement do the job? Well, try to think of something simpler— there usually is something. Then, when the tests are running, we look for duplication and simplify the entire system as far as possible. This final simplification process is called *Refactoring* (page 76).

Now, with the tests all running and the code simplified, we're ready to release the code. That can be a moderately complex process, and we talk about it in some detail in *Releasing Changes* (page 121). The basic ideas are simple: keep the unit tests at 100 percent, so there are no regressions; release often, so that there will be few collisions from people editing the same classes; re-sync with the rest of the team, so that the system stays in continuous integration; and use a single point of integration to serialize updates. Good XP pairs release software many times per day and retest the integrated system every time. The less time you wait, the fewer problems you'll have.

There you have it. Task done, built by a pair of programmers, testing first, expressing intention, maintaining a simple design through starting simply and refactoring as needed, following an agreed-upon coding standard, and releasing code frequently to keep everyone notching forward together. Check out some important details below.

Collective Code Ownership

I'm not afraid to change my own code. And it's all my own code.

As you work with code, you'll inevitably find that there's behavior you need on objects that you weren't planning to work on. You'll always find that there's commonality between what you're working on and some other object you weren't thinking about when you started. You'll always find behavior on one object that belongs somewhere else. You'll find objects that you were planning to work with that are recalcitrant, somehow resisting your attempts to use them. What should you do?

Well, if you owned those objects, you'd just fix them, wouldn't you? Yuck, this is wrong, you'd think. Let's fix it. Whack, wham, a little refactoring, and now it's all better. Then you'd move on.

If you didn't own those objects, it'd be a different story. You'd have to find the owner, explain your problem, talk him into the need for the change, wait for him to whine and complain about how much he has to do, and wait again while he gets around to making the changes you need. Then, of course, they wouldn't be quite right, either because he didn't understand—or because you didn't.

The first way is better. Therefore, own everything. There you are, and your problem is solved. If an object needs to help you, own it, and make it help you. If its interface isn't quite right, own it and fix it. If it doesn't have quite enough power in some method, own it, and beef it up. If it doesn't inherit the right stuff, own it, and move it.

Life is better if you own everything. There's just one drawback: it wouldn't be fair to all the other programmers if you didn't let them own everything, too. So all the programmers own all the code. Now, we're just down to the details of how.

Simple Design

Simplicity is more complicated than you think. But it's well worth it.

We all strive for simple and clear design, don't we? Of course we do. But in XP, we take it to extremes. At every moment in time, we want the system to be as simple as possible. That means that we want no additional functions that aren't used, no structures or algorithms that are more complex than the current need would dictate.

As programmers, we pride ourselves on our ability to predict what "they're gonna need," and we like to put in generality looking forward to that day. Extreme programmers don't do that. The best don't do that, ever. Isn't that risky? Won't it be harder to put in later? Well, no, it isn't risky, and no, it won't be harder to put in later. Here's why: if you keep the system simple enough at all times, then whatever you put in will go in easily and in as few places as possible. Here's what we mean by simple enough. Our code is simple enough when it

1. Runs all the tests
2. Expresses every idea you need to express
3. Contains no duplicate code
4. Has the minimum number of classes and methods

Let's think about the implications of this a bit. If there is no duplicated code, then whatever needs changing is in just one place, cornered, where it'll be easy to change. Therefore, adding needed generality or enhancements will be easy. If the code runs the tests and has the minimum number of classes or methods, then there is nothing in it that is unused. Therefore, it is efficient and dedicated to exactly what it has to do right now. If the code expresses every idea we need to express, we'll be able to find the concepts we need (like *totalSalary*) when we look for them.

Code written like this, tested intensely, very expressive, free of duplication, and of minimal size, is a delight to work with. It's a delight to write as well, and of all the joys of XP, seeing this craftsmanlike simple code emerge is one of the greatest.

To keep the code this way, we have to become good at refactoring.

Refactoring

We keep the code simple at all times. This minimizes investment in excess framework and support code. We retain the necessary flexibility through refactoring.

Refactoring is the process of improving the code's structure while preserving its function. The definitive book on the subject is Martin Fowler's *Refactoring: Improving the Design of Existing Code*. Get it, study it, and learn it. We can't begin to do it justice here, but we'll tell you a bit about how and why.

Even if you spent a lot of time designing up front, as you wouldn't do on an XP project, the details of your design would inevitably be wrong here and there. If you focus on delivering business value rapidly, your system will have an even greater need to evolve. Refactoring is what keeps you from getting wedged in by your own changes. Have you ever needed a new way to do something in the code, implemented it, and then put off updating all the existing uses of the old way? Well, probably not, but we have, and we can tell you that it leads to code that is hard to understand, hard to update, and contains duplication. Since you've probably never done it, don't start.

Instead, when the design wants to change, as it will, change it. Put in the new capability you need; move the functionality to the class where it wants to be; create the new helper class that's called for. Then bring the entire system into line using the new capability, just as if it had been there all the time. Nothing else is really good enough—everything else leaves you with cruft growing on your code.

Refactoring is a formal process (but not a difficult one) that lets you change the code without breaking it. Each refactoring step is reversible, so that you can try things and if you don't like the outcome, you can put them back. This lets you have a curious, experimental, learning attitude about your code. Hmm, this seems a bit off, let's refactor it this way. Oh, that's better. We'll leave it. Or, um, that's not so good, let's put it back.

Through refactoring and focus on simple design, we can build a system incrementally, focused on business value, without getting cornered by an early decision that turns out to be wrong. We expect our early decisions to need updating, and through refactoring, we know just how to do it. Read Martin's book and learn refactoring. It's a critical skill in these times of rapid change.

One more thing: one reason people don't change existing code is that they're afraid they'll break it. But you have all those unit tests that ran at 100 percent when you started. When you're finished with a little refactoring, run them again. If they break, see what happened. Most likely, you broke something, although sometimes you'll just find that the test needed changing to match the refactoring. The tests are your safety net, protecting you from breaking the system during fast evolution. Just don't tell anyone we have a safety net—they wouldn't let us call it Extreme Programming if they knew we work with a net.

Continuous Integration

Integration is a bear. We can't put it off forever. Let's do it all the time instead.

Here's an idea. Let's divide up the system. We'll all write our share of the objects. It should take only a few months. We'll all test our work. Then, when everything is written, we'll just integrate the code in a week or so, run a few acceptance tests, and release.

Does this sound like a recipe for disaster, with mismatched method signatures, objects that don't work as their users expected, and a system that won't even load, let alone actually run? We sure hope it sounds that bad.

The longer we wait between integrations and acceptance tests, the worse things get. Wait twice as long and we'll have four or more times the hassle. The reason is that one bug written just yesterday is pretty easy to find, while ten or a hundred written weeks ago can become almost impossible.

The Extreme solution, of course, is to integrate as often as possible. We call it *continuous integration*. A good XP team will integrate and test the entire system many times per day. Yes, many times per day.

Most of us have worked on systems with a zillion lines of code that took hours to compile and link. The authors once met with a team whose system took a week to build. The system in question was smaller than ours, which took ten minutes to build on a bad day.

Well, if your system already takes ages to build, you're on your own. You'll have to get it down any way you can. But if you're starting clean, it's really quite easy.

Build many times a day. If the build starts getting slow, get right on it. Keep inter-file dependencies low. Set up your make dependencies to keep as many files as possible in object form except when they're actually edited. Use dynamic loading where possible. Build intermediate partially linked object files. Build lots of DLLs wherever possible. Experiment with different structures, learn what works best. But above all, keep build time low.

Keep after it. Effort spent improving the build is more than repaid in reduced integration hassles.

Work toward continuous integration. And while you're at it, keep the unit tests fast.

Coding Standard

I can always read my own code. But wait, it's all my own code.

We all code to an agreed coding standard. This ensures that the code communicates as clearly as possible and supports our shared responsibility for quality everywhere. It doesn't matter so much what the standard is. What's more important is that everyone use it. Yes, we know it sounds regimented at first, but it will pay off. Suppose someone went onto your computer some night and reformatted all your code. Not only would you change your password, but you'd be slowed down. You might even go to the trouble to format it all back because you need to be able to just glance at the code and see what it's up to.

Now, it turns out that it isn't the specifics of your favorite formatting that matter; it's your familiarity with them. So push a bit for your favorite style but be prepared to bend and go with the team's choices. In a very short time, if you use the new style, you'll get just as good at it as you are with your favorite. You may even come to like the other style better. No, really, it happened to us.

Now, what about the specifics? Easy and simpler is better. If you're programming in Smalltalk, our advice is to adopt Kent Beck's *Best Practice Smalltalk Patterns* as a whole. They're thoughtful, consistent, and simple. If you're not lucky enough to be programming in Smalltalk, you're on your own. Look for some industry or local standards in your language, and adopt those. Here are some key topics we'd think about in our standard:

Indentation. Use a consistent indentation format. Same tab widths all the time, same bracket placement. Always indent subordinate code, even if you're not using Python, where you have to.

Capitalization. Use consistent capitalization practices. Follow what's typical in your language, not something left over from another language, even if you're more familiar with it. Do they capitalize classes and put underbars in their names? OK, go with it.

Commenting. Use sparse commenting. A focus on clear, intention-revealing code is more valuable than all the comments you can write.

Do write them when you need them—to explain an optimization, to explain something you just can't simplify, and so on. Don't write them when they don't really help.

Method size. Keep methods small. If the code can't be seen in one display screen, it's too long. It's probably too long anyway. While you're at it, avoid those big comment blocks at the beginning of the method—they obscure what matters, the actual code.

Names. There is another area of standardization that you want to work on throughout the project, and that's the names themselves. Even though your name formats will be consistent, the names of things will want to be consistent as well. It's not helpful if you call it totalSalary and I call it totPay. We need to name things similarly so that we can find them, and so we can understand them quickly when we see them. The impact of consistent naming is small at first, when the system is trivial, but as things get bigger and you learn to go faster, having consistent names helps keep you going at full speed. It's well worth the investment.

Use names that communicate, not ones that are convenient to type. Longer is better, within reason. The idea is that your code needs to communicate with you, and with your colleagues, in the future, when you've forgotten what "pig" and "cow" meant to you at the time. For further ideas on this, read Ward Cunningham's *System of Names*, http://c2.com/cgi/wiki?SystemOfNames, or the names discussion in Hunt and Thomas's *Pragmatic Programmer*, or go back to the classics.

In XP we call this concept *Metaphor*, the idea that each application should have a conceptual integrity based on a simple metaphor that everyone understands, explaining the essence of how the program works. The essence of this idea is to have a common concept of what the program is "like." C3 payroll, for example, is like a manufacturing line, building paychecks by taking hour parts and converting them to dollar parts, assembling all the various parts until you get a paycheck. Odd as it may seem, this metaphor let the customer and programmers communicate clearly about what the system does and how it does it.

Creating a good metaphor for your program is something we can't yet teach you to do—we manage to do it about half the time we try. It's a brainstorming process that, when it succeeds, gives you a basis for creating names for all the objects in your program and gives you a clear way of describing its operation to programmers and humans alike. Suddenly, a program that seemed mysterious and complex becomes clear and simple. Get creative. When you have the right metaphor, it will click. On the other hand, if your general ledger program just looks like general ledger to you, or your air traffic control program doesn't look like an ant colony, move on, and build conceptual integrity some other way. When we are able to say more about metaphor, you can be sure that we will.

Forty-Hour Week

One time on the authors' C3 project, the entire team went into a heavy overtime mode in order to meet some delivery date. (Yes, even Extreme teams can get up against a deadline once in a while. Scope had not been managed properly, and we were up against it.) We worked really hard for a few weeks. Most of the team were coming in on weekends, in the middle of the night, and generally acting like we were in Silicon Valley instead of Michigan.

After the crunch was over, we all took some time off and then got back to it. We looked upon the work we had done in the overtime period, and unlike the Creator, we did not see that it was good. In fact, it was bad.[1] We found poorly written code, we found untested code, and we found unrefactored code. We found all pig iron.

During the crunch, we were honestly doing our best. Our best just wasn't very good, because we were tired. We can't prove it yet,[2] but from our own experience we are certain that heavy overtime is bad. Thus the XP rule of the Forty-Hour Week: Do not work more than one consecutive week of overtime.

---

1. We offer apologies here to our wise and more gentle colleague, Don Wells, (http://www.extremeprogramming.org), who doesn't like to call work done with the best of will "bad." Suffice it to say that we looked upon what we had wrought and did not see that it was good.

2. We can't prove it yet, but we're working on it. Recent research has shown that the commong hospital practice of overworking residents and interns results in more mistakes than letting them work more normal hours. Don't forget that the next time you go to the hospital and the next time you decide to program while you're tired.

Summary

Of course programming is what it's all about. XP embeds programming in a process that lets programmers stay healthy through the course of a project, by helping the project to stay healthy. As we program, we work in pairs, using simple design plus refactoring to keep design quality high. We integrate all the time, so that we can all improve the code wherever it needs improving. And we communicate through the code by writing in a meaningful, standard way.

Code Quality

A little more detail on something close to our hearts: simplicity.

Remember when code is "simple enough." Everything we write must

1. Run all the tests
2. Express every idea that we need to express
3. Say everything once and only once
4. Have the minimum number of classes and methods consistent with the above

Run All the Tests

It's most important that the code does what it has to do. In XP, there is only one way to know whether the code does what it has to do: there must be a test. A feature does not exist unless there is a test for it.

Does this mean that every class must have tests? Not necessarily, but it wouldn't hurt. If a class has no behavior that could possibly break, then it doesn't need tests. If it could possibly break, test it.

What if another class uses ours, and the other class has tests? Does our class need tests? More likely than not, it does. Does the test for the other class test every feature of our class? Probably it does not. Will our class ever need enhancement or clarification or optimization? Probably it will. Changing our class and testing it by running other people's tests isn't very well targeted.

Most classes need tests for anything that could possibly break. Writing those tests, you'll find problems sooner and the project will go faster. Writing the tests first will make our classes easier to use and more compact.

The code we release must run all the tests. It's not sufficient that the tests for our code run—all the tests in the entire system must still run whenever we release. This ensures that changes we make don't impact other people in surprising ways.

Express Every Idea

As we write code, we are thinking. (We'll assume that, anyway.) As we go along, we think:

I have to turn all these strings into operands . . . turning this string into an operand I have to see whether it starts with an operator . . . an operator is a plus or a minus . . . or it might not have one . . . if it has one, the rest of the string is the variable name . . . if it doesn't, the whole string is the variable name. . . .

At the end of coding, the program should clearly express all of those ideas. Yes, I know they're all there, embedded in our loops and nested if statements. But they are hidden. Instead, let every idea be expressed explicitly in the code.

Say Everything Once and Only Once

Whenever code is duplicated, get rid of it. Make a method of it, make an object to do it, do something. Get rid of it.

Where there is duplicated code, there is usually an idea lurking: first I'll convert this one, then I'll convert that one. That idea needs to be expressed.

Where there is duplicated code, there is always an opportunity to make the program smaller. Do it.

Where there is duplicated code, there is always an opportunity for one of the duplicates to get fixed and the other one to be forgotten. Remove this opportunity.

Where there is duplicated code, there is more code to read before you understand the program. Make the job easier.

Hmm . . . there's duplication above. I should have said:

When there is duplicated code:

- There is usually an idea lurking: first I'll convert this one, then I'll convert that one. Express that idea.
- There is always a way to make the program smaller. Do it.
- There is always a chance for one of the duplicates to get fixed and the other one to be forgotten. Remove this chance.
- There is more code to read and understand. Make your job easier.

Minimize Number of Classes and Methods

When all these things are done, if there are classes and methods we no longer need, remove them. This won't happen very often—programming with tests first and then expressing each intention once and only once generally minimizes classes and methods.

We put this rule here to remind ourselves that it is last. Minimize classes and methods but not at the expense of correctness, expressiveness, or duplication of code.

Chapter 12

Pair Programming

On an Extreme Programming team, two programmers sitting together at the same machine write all production code.

Pair programming has been around for ages. We've heard that P. J. Plauger wrote about working in pairs back in the '70s, perhaps in one of his "Programming on Purpose" columns, but we haven't been able to find the reference. Nearly everyone has had the experience of working together with another programmer on something really difficult, or on a really serious emergency, and it's usually a good experience.

With pair programming, as with most of XP, we turn the dials up to ten. We don't reserve pair programming for difficult problems or for serious emergencies. We do it all the time—all production code, all the time.

Two programmers working together generate more code, and better code, than the same two programmers working separately. They can work longer without getting tired, and when they're finished, two people understand everything, instead of understanding just half of everything.[1]

A cat is not a dog, we are told, and pair programming isn't one programmer looking over another's shoulder as she bangs in code. Pair programming is two programmers, side by side, working together to write the program. The programmer currently doing the typing is called the driver, and the other is called the partner. The partner isn't sitting idly by, but is actively engaged and helping every minute.

When you are typing in a method definition, you are spinning a lot of dishes at once. You have an intention in mind for the method—it is supposed to accomplish some task. You are trying to type legal statements of the programming language, keeping the syntax rules in mind. You are trying to type meaningful code, code that can be understood now, and that will be understood months or years from now. You are trying to conform to the team's coding standards. You are sending messages to other objects, requiring you to remember what they are and what messages they understand. All of this is fitting into an overall context of what you are trying to accomplish, and all of it has to be spelled and punctuated correctly. No wonder we make so many mistakes. It's a wonder we can program at all.

Your experience may vary, but what I (Ron) can keep well in mind is usually just the purpose of the method, the general algorithm I have in

---

1. We're not just making this up. Experiments in pair programming show its benefits. See, for example, Laurie Williams and Robert Kessler's article in the May 2000 *Communications of the ACM (CACM)*.

mind, and most of the syntax rules of the language. If I need to think about anything else, I have to kind of swap out one of those items and swap in something else, like the protocol of some object I'm talking to. Every time I make that mental swap, I have a chance of losing a little bit of my picture. It slows me down, and once in a while I even make a mistake. On the average, I make at least one mistake requiring an edit (a backspace or worse) in every method I write. I almost always need to reformat or rename variables, though some of that can be done after the method works.

My partner keeps track of the things I don't have in my brain. Because he doesn't have to think so hard about just what the method is, he spots simple errors like spelling and punctuation. Because he is tracking carefully with where we're going, he reminds me of the message protocol to the objects I'm dealing with, and he makes sure I'm not going off down some rat hole, implementing something we don't even need. As I move from method to method, he makes sure our strategy is consistent and reminds me of the names of the methods and variables we've just defined. Finally, my partner acts as the pair's conscience, reminding us to keep the code communicative, to keep it formatted to the team's standards, and to keep it tested.

Both driver and partner have responsibilities during pair programming.

The partner is responsible for being completely engaged. He's not just along for the ride; he must understand everything that is being done. If he doesn't, he needs to stop the process and get hooked up again.

The partner must be working the same strategy as the driver. He might have another idea, he might even think it is better. Tough. When you're the partner, your job is to help the driver do what the driver is doing. Get with what's going on and support it.

The driver, in addition to typing in the code, is responsible for making sure that the partner is completely engaged. The driver explains what she is doing, so the partner can understand it. She also listens to what the partner is saying and to what he is not saying. If she stops hearing encouraging noises from her partner, she needs to stop and see what's wrong. If she hears discouraging noises, she needs to stop even sooner.

We're trying to build a mind-meld here, and both players need to keep it going.

It takes a little time to get used to pair programming, and, at first, it will feel a bit awkward. Then you'll get good at pairing with someone, and finally you'll get good at pairing with most anyone. Just keep at it. Here are some tips:

The partner can say, "Let me drive," when he can't express an idea verbally, or when the driver is stuck. It's a good idea to switch drivers every so often anyway, just to keep from getting stale.

It's generally best if the programmer who is least sure of what's being done does most of the driving. It's easy to let yourself get sucked along when you don't really get it, and then you lose the advantage of pairing.

When you're the driver, notice all the times your partner helps. Acknowledge them to yourself and to him. Sometimes it'll just be syntax or punctuation help. Sometimes he'll remind you of the method name you were trying to remember or point to the window button you're looking for. Sometimes he'll remind you to write a test that you need or remind you that the code isn't communicating as well as it could. Notice these aids and acknowledge them.

As partner, learn your driver's rhythm. Don't prompt every time before he's ready. Just prompt when he's a bit stuck. Try to speak in "we" terms rather than "you" terms, especially when what you have to say isn't entirely favorable. "We need to make that variable name a bit more clear."

Speak in "I" terms when the going gets tough. Is the driver writing something grotesquely ugly, the least understandable code you've ever seen? Then just say, "I don't understand that. Can you help me out? Let's make it better."

Partner, don't take the driver off his strategy unless you really need to. If you do, try something like this: "I've got an idea. Let's try it that way for five minutes. Then I'd like to try something."

Driver, don't run away with what you're doing. Chances are, your partner does have a better idea because, while you've been down in the mud, he's had his head up above the ground looking around. Listen.

We can't offer much more detail than that. Each pair is unique, but the general moves are the same. Work at pairing. The result will be more code, better code, better understanding of the system, and more fun.

Pair programming, if you can do it, will make you go faster in any situation. In *Software Development* (October 1999), Larry Constantine put it this way:

They spell each other, check each other's work, inspire each other, fill in each other's weak spots, and crank out better code with fewer defects. The same formula works for learning a language or using a new piece of software— you not only learn from the system or the material but from each other. A dynamic duo who work well together can be worth three people working in isolation.

Pairing doesn't come naturally to everyone, but most folks get to like it once they try it. Here are some techniques for getting started:

Ask for help by pairing. This is a powerful approach to many problems, and a wonderful one for pairing since it lets the other person be the strong one. "Jack, could you sit down and help me for a couple of minutes?" Next thing you know, you're pairing.

Provide help by pairing. When someone asks you how something works, or how to do something, try saying "I've got a few minutes. Let's take a look at it." Move to his machine, give him the keyboard, and help him through it.

Send help by pairing. After folks get used to working with you, encourage other pairs to get together: "Susan, could you sit with Jim on that and help him with those formats? I'll join you if you need me."

Drop in. Just plunk down at the desk of people who look confused. "Whatcha' doin'?"

Finally, remember that desk or table layout is critical for pair programming. Computer in the inside corner doesn't work. Two chairs side by side facing the monitor, that's the ticket.

Summary

Two programmers working together are more effective than two working alone. Team knowledge grows faster and the work is more fun.

Chapter 13

Unit Tests

Extreme Programmers test everything that could possibly break,
using automated tests that must run perfectly all the time.

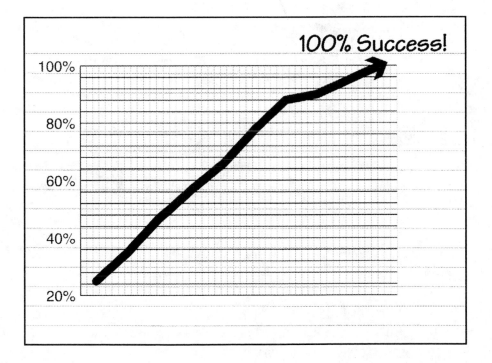

In order to deliver value as early as possible, XP teams work only on what the customer orders. They refine the design and code continually so the system is always clean and capable of evolving. Code refinement is possible only if you have lots of tests to prove that things still work. Therefore, XP teams build automated unit tests for everything, and make sure they run perfectly all the time.

XP teams share ownership of all classes. This lets them go quickly, with no waiting for someone else to get around to putting in a needed feature. When code is being changed rapidly, you need to know you haven't broken anything. Therefore, XP teams build automated tests for everything, and make sure they run perfectly all the time.

Let's be clear about this: you need tests for every class—for everything that could possibly break. And all those tests must run at 100 percent all the time.

Imagine that you had just been brought in to maintain an application of a thousand or so classes, 10,000 methods, and 50,000 lines of code. The former team have all run off to join the circus. You might be feeling some fear about now. Then your manager tells you one more thing: "Oh, by the way, there are about 10,000 tests for the system, testing all the classes and important methods, and every one of them runs correctly." We hope this would give you some comfort. We know it would give us comfort.

It turns out that if it's your own 10,000 methods and 50,000 lines of code, the tests will give you the same comfort. So we want tests for everything, and we want them to run perfectly all the time. How do we do that?

It helps to start at the beginning. We'll address later what to do when you have a bunch of code to maintain and not enough tests. Starting on a new project, you can have all the tests you will need by writing them as you go. And you'll go faster when you work that way, a wonderful additional benefit.

The best way to write tests for a class is to write them first—test a little, code a little—rather than writing them at the end, or even writing them all at the beginning. All of these ways will result in what you need, but going bit by bit is best. We'll focus on that.

Testing Bit by Bit

There's a full example on this in *Test First, by Intention* on page 107. Check that out for some detailed ideas. Here we'll just give you the basics, and we'll assume that you're using a testing framework like xUnit (page 105), our favorite testing tool.

OK, you have decided you need a class to hold a collection of completed tax returns. It has to be able to give back a collection of all the returns whose "score" is larger than a user-supplied number, and it has to be able to remove all the returns whose score is less than some other number. It should be able to accept the addition of new forms. This class, of course, will be driven by the tax auditor's GUI that Bill is working on with his partner, and it will use the return scoring capability that Martha is building with hers.

We'll even suppose that Martha isn't done with the tax return objects, and certainly we aren't going to work with the GUI. Our mission is just to write the Tax Return Scrutinizer.

We want to build up our tests, bit by bit. We'll first test to see if we can create a Scrutinizer with no elements, and that it behaves reasonably. Our first test, therefore, just creates a Scrutinizer. Then we ask it some questions: "Give me all the returns scoring more than 10." It should answer an empty collection. We ask it to remove all the returns scoring less than five. It should happily accept this command, removing none of its already absent returns.

We create a test case in xUnit, named *ScrutinizerTestCase,* and write a test that looks like this:

```
testEmpty
    create a new Scrutinizer
    select returns with score > 10
    result size should be zero
    remove returns with score < 5
    nothing should blow up
```

Then we run the test. Depending on your programming language, you may have to define the *Scrutinizer* class or maybe even some of its methods. Be sure to define the methods from the point of view of the user, i.e., your test. This is a good chance to make them easy to use.

Finally, the test can run. Probably it will run correctly. If it doesn't (maybe you forgot to initialize the Scrutinizer's return collection), fix it.

The test works, and we move on to another one. Let's test adding returns. But wait, there aren't any, because Martha isn't finished! What shall we do? I just asked Chet, and he said, "We'll make a fake one." That's right, we're just here to implement and test the Scrutinizer, and we can test it without having any real returns to test. So create a stub class called *FakeTaxReturn,* give it a constructor method, and write your test to add them in.

```
testAdding
    create a scrutinizer
    add some fake returns with various scores
    see how many returns the scrutinizer has
```

The test for adding needs to find out how many returns are in the Scrutinizer. We might have done that in the first test, but it wasn't on our mind, because we knew that a new Scrutinizer has no returns. Size seems like a reasonable thing for it to be able to answer, so we'll just implement a public size method and move on. In rare cases you might need to build a friend method or do something a little more exotic. Generally, it can be this simple, and we recommend that you keep it that way.

OK, now we want to test the selection. No problem, just extend the *FakeTaxReturn* to have a score, and use it in a test. This would be a good time to coordinate with Martha on the name of the method, so we'll use the same name here and in the real *TaxReturn*. Our test is easy: add a few returns of various scores, ask for returns with scores bigger than X, and see if we get the right number of returns.

```
testSelecting
    create a scrutinizer
    add some fake returns with various scores
    select all the returns with score > 10
    see if you get the right number
    select all the returns with score > 5
    see if you get the right number.
```

Some people might not be satisfied just checking the number of returns. They'd want to look at the result collection and see whether it contained the exact expected returns. Do this if it makes you comfortable, but if, by inspection, you can see that if the code gets the right number of returns it must have the right returns, there's no need to test further.

Here's an important point: you are trying to test everything that could possibly break in this object. If you can see from the code that if it selects a return correctly it will return it correctly, then there's no need to dig further. Use judgment, of course, but there's no need to go nuts. There's more on this in *Everything That Could Possibly Break* (page 233).

Now we're in good shape to test the removal. We have enough mechanism here to write the test, except for the removal method itself. Add a few returns, select some, remove the ones less than some number, check to see how many are left, check some selections to see if you get the (new) right answer. Run the test, and watch it fail until you fix the removal mechanism. We won't show the test pseudocode this time, you can certainly visualize it by now.

Inch by inch, step by step, we test and build our way to a running class. When we've got it doing everything we want, we're ready to release the tests and the code.

That's right, tests and code. Now that we have written these tests, we don't throw them away or file them for future use. We immediately make them permanent parts of the system. We release our new test case and our new classes to the version control system. That's discussed in more detail in *Releasing Changes* on page 121. But here's a short summary:

Everyone on the team releases code only when all the unit tests in the entire system run at 100 percent. This is a critical point about XP, so we'll repeat it: in the released code, all the unit tests must run at 100 percent all the time. When we put our Scrutinizer code away, with all tests at 100 percent, we're sure that everything works in the whole system. When we come back later and add some more new tests and code, then run the whole suite and something breaks, we know that only our changes could have broken it. If we've only worked for a little while between releases, we'll have no difficulty finding the problem.

The effect of all this is that the system kind of notches forward in correctness. Each time a pair of programmers releases a few more tests and a bit more code, the system becomes more complete, and more correct at the same time. Using this approach, you'll rarely, if ever, get those embarrassing regressions where you release what was supposed to be a simple change and the whole system goes weird.

The feeling of confidence that comes from building tests for everything, together with the code, is one of the best parts of XP. Be sure to experience it for yourself.

One more point on the Scrutinizer test, then we'll move on to some more general unit testing questions. We used a *FakeTaxReturn* to make sure that the Scrutinizer worked, without having to wait for Martha to get the real *TaxReturn* object working. That leaves a small crack in the system, the possibility that Martha will name the method that returns the score something other than "score." A case could be made that the Scrutinizer should be tested with real *TaxReturns* as well.

We'd agree with that, but there are two key points to consider on the other side. First of all, we don't want to have programmers waiting on each other. That just slows things down. You'll naturally try to order your tasks to prevent that from happening, but things work fine if you just go ahead. Second, with more complex collaborating objects than the Scrutinizer, you can get strange interactions in your testing. We often find that using stub objects instead of the real thing will simplify the testing and help you go faster.

But it's important not to lose track of the connection between the assumed method name and the real one. There are several good approaches. Pick one that applies best in the actual situation.

1. You might find it desirable to write a task on the board to write at least one test for Scrutinizer using real returns when that's possible.
2. If Martha hasn't even started the *TaxReturn* object yet, create the class yourself, give it the necessary method to answer the score, and use it in the test. Now when Martha gets started on *TaxReturn*, she'll find the method and tests, and she'll work to preserve the semantics. It's worth mentioning to the team that you're creating the *TaxReturn* object, so everyone will know to look for it.
3. If *TaxReturn* exists, you could check it out, implement "score," and check it back in. If Martha has it checked out at the moment, she'll get a collision when she goes to release, but the integration will be trivial. Of course, you'll give her a heads-up that you're doing it anyway.
4. You could write a test that uses reflection to see whether there is a *TaxReturn* class, and if there is, whether it responds to the score method. If it doesn't, fail the test. This is a bit glitzy for the example and you'll have to wear the propeller beanie, but for a more complex situation, it can be very worthwhile. If every subclass of some master class must have its own implementation of "foo," for example, a unit test that checks them all can be a lifesaver.

Having discussed all these options, we now think that the *Fake-TaxReturn* wasn't the best possible idea. Probably creating the class or editing it would have been better in this case, because it would have required less human coordination instead of relying on the source code and the version control system to keep things in order. We decided to leave the example this way, however, because it gave us a basis for the discussion of the options. Sometimes you get lucky.

Summary of Testing Steps

Here, in a nutshell, is a sketch of unit testing the XP way:

1. Create a test class. Name it in such a way as to evoke the class or process you will be testing. If you are testing the *Scrutinizer* class, call the test class *ScrutinizerTestCase*.
2. Code a setup method to create a *Scrutinizer* object. You may find the need to add example creation methods to the tested class to aid in the setup. Be sure to test this code, as an error in this type of code can be very difficult to debug later.
3. Write a test. If your new behavior will change the state of the *Scrutinizer* instance, code an assertion to verify its current state. Then send the message for your new behavior to the *Scrutinizer* instance. If you don't know the message selector, now is the time to make one up. Depending on your implementation language, you may need to code a stub method. Now code an assertion to verify that your expected change in state occurred.
4. Run the test. It will probably fail. If it does not, you are done. All that is left to do is release. Go to step six.
5. Modify the model code and repeat steps four and five until the test runs successfully.
6. Release the model code and the test case.

Testing Questions

Now here are some questions that get asked every time we talk about this subject, so we're guessing that you'll have some or all of them. If we miss yours, drop us an e-mail.

How Do You Test When You Have an Attached Database?

There are a couple of things to be concerned about when testing with an attached database. First of all may be performance. We need the unit tests to run really fast, so that we can do our test code release cycle as quickly as possible. If lots of unit tests rely on the database, it can slow the tests down. That causes programmers to release less frequently, which increases collisions in the code manager, which slows you down even more. That's bad. Keep the database-related tests fast.

The basic trick is to write most of the tests that use data from the database to use data from files, or from memory, instead. Just capture the database result, as records or objects, and write it to a file in the test directories. Then write the tests to use the file data instead of going to the database. Often this is best done by having a dummy database object, perhaps one that looks at the SQL statement it receives and just opens the corresponding data file. Other times, you can test using the data without needing to fake out the database.

But you do need to test the database access as well. Having just a few tests that actually open the database and get records from it, making sure that the connection works, that the records come back right, and so on, is a really good idea. Then try to make those tests as tight as possible.

You might feel the need to test your record-mapping methods, the ones that take the stuff that comes back from the database and turns it into objects. These tests can be written against hard-coded data as well, but it might be a good idea to have one that runs against the real database, just in case a version changes (or something) and they start sending you data in a different format.

The basic rule is to go to the actual database as infrequently as possible, consonant with safety, so that the tests run as rapidly as possible.

What if Your Tests Run Really Slowly?

This is a big deal, as we mentioned above. Slow tests slow down the entire project. The short answer is to optimize them. If you have a profiler, run it on the tests. You'll invariably find two things: tests that are doing more than they need to and parts of the system that are too slow. Fix the system parts that are too slow—you have the tests there to let you optimize with confidence—and gain two benefits: a faster system and faster tests.

Tests that do too much should be fixed as well. Are you running an entire paycheck to see whether the tax deduction is correctly taken? Take a little more time in setup and just check the one object that's involved.

And, of course, look for things like excessive use of an external resource, such as a database or other remote connection.

What if You Can't Figure Out How to Test a Class?

This is often a good sign that there's something odd about the class. Clearly we can't give specific advice without seeing the class, but the guidelines are always the same.

Is the class hard to create? This is often due to not having, or not following, a coding standard that calls for a complete constructor method. Taking the time to make the object easier to build will probably help.

Does the class being tested collaborate with a lot of other complex objects that are hard to get? This is a hint that you need some stub objects to work with, and it also suggests that the class might benefit from a little refactoring to make it less dependent on so many others.

Get with the team and talk about what's hard to test. You'll think of something most every time. And better tests make you go faster—you'll be glad you did.

Is It OK to Test a Class by Just Testing the Classes that Use It?

There's more discussion on this in *Everything That Could Possibly Break* (page 233), but lean away from this. It's true that if the using classes exercise the "inner" class enough, all the defects will show up. But there are two serious drawbacks to this approach. First of all, the limitations of the inner class may not be exercised by its users, but may show up in production. It's better to do a little "white box" testing, looking directly at the inner class and exercising it directly.

Second, when the other tests fail due to an error in the inner guy, you'll have a bit more of a debugging session to fix it. Think of it this way: if you have a test that says the square root of four should be two, and the test fails, you will know it's the square root that broke. If you have a numeric routine that relies, among many other things, on getting correct square roots, you could debug for a long time before noticing that the root is wrong. Local tests give better diagnostics, so you go faster.

How Do You Know You Have Tested Everything that Could Possibly Break?

We have a chapter on that very subject, *Everything That Could Possibly Break* (page 233). The short answer is that it's a matter of conscience—

really trying—and experience. When the software gets an error in an acceptance test, it's a sign that a unit test was missing. Write that test, then think about what it reminds you of. Write all those tests, too. You'll quickly get good at this.

When the software gets an error in the users' hands, you have a sign that you need both acceptance and unit test enhancements. Learn from this yourselves, in terms of what kinds of tests are needed. And help the software learn as well, by writing the new ones you need right now.

What Do you Do if You Have a Body of Already Written Code, but not Many Tests?

I suppose running away isn't an option. There are changes that need to be made, since if there aren't, you might as well work on something else. Figure out what part of the system the changes are going to affect, and write tests around that part. If you're working on a defect, always write the test that shows the defect first. Then write tests that relate to it, tests that you are reminded of by the one that actually finds the bug.

At first, it seems as if the tests slow you down. But the first time you release something that doesn't work, and feel like a fool, remember this section. Build a scaffolding of tests before you work. It'll help keep the walls from coming down while you rebuild them.

What about Errors that Show Up Only in Collaborations Between Classes?

Our Scrutinizer problem above gave an example of how a collaboration error could show up, and we discussed how to avoid it. If your system is showing lots of such errors, there's some kind of coordination problem happening. People are writing different responses to the same questions, or they are naming classes and methods inconsistently, or there are consistency checks needed in the unit tests, or something. When this kind of error shows up, it's a sign that some additional work needs to be done. All we can say is that you need to figure out what that work is and do it. Since these defects are hard to find, when they start showing up, it's time to invest in cornering them.

Our own experience is that we get very few of these errors. We're guessing here, but we think that somehow our focus on testing up front is preventing them, although we can't prove it. And we certainly agree that when they do show up, such problems are difficult to find. So when they show up, we go after them vigorously by trying to build a tighter net of tests around those areas.

What About Real-Time Errors or Multithreading Errors?

These can be very problematical. Real-time and multithreading errors are not very amenable to testing. Our basic reaction is to do the simplest designs possible in these areas and to make sure that lots of eyes look at them. When errors do occur, it's often possible to write tests, especially reflective ones, that ensure that all objects that do X are first synchronizing on X's semaphore, and such. We'd write them, and we recommend that you do so as well.

What about GUIs?

Arrgh, GUI testing. The basic rule is this: do no processing in your GUI code. No logic is needed other than the inherent event logic of press this, change these widgets to contain that.

Everything else should be done in model code, where it is easy to test. All the selections for the list boxes, and so on. Everything. The rule is simple: the model is easy to test; the GUI is not. So make the GUI simple and test the model vigorously.

To check whether the GUIs respond correctly, there are those click-recording GUI testing tools out there. All the ones we have used were equally good and equally awkward. Try them, and pick one that works for you.

My Stuff Can't Be Tested Because . . .

We don't believe you. We think you can test anything. It helps if you start that way and stay that way, because when you write a little tiny thing that "can't" be tested and then make it testable, the system never gets away from you. Test, then code, then test, then code. You'll be glad you did.

xUnit

Use the world's lightest testing tool.

Starting with unit tests is a bit difficult—you just don't know what to do. Here's some free software to give you a leg up.

Kent Beck wrote a testing framework, called SUnit, for Smalltalk some years ago. It caught on all over, especially in XP teams using Smalltalk. He and Erich Gamma then provided the JUnit tool for Java. Today there are CppUnit, PerlUnit, PyUnit for Python, VBUnit for Visual Basic, and many other languages as well. These frameworks are available on Ron Jeffries' web site, www.XProgramming.com.[1] Click the "software" link.

Within the limitations of the language being tested, all the frameworks work the same way. You build a subclass of the class *TestCase* to contain your tests for some object that needs testing. (And they all do.)

The test case includes as many testing methods as you want. Typically, each one begins with *test*. They might be named *testCreation*, *testSelection*, *testRemoval*, and so forth. The versions of the tool in languages with reflection build up test suites automatically, by collecting all the methods named *test* . . . . In less advanced languages, you have to set up the suites manually.

The testing framework collects up all the tests and executes them one after another. Each one is initialized by calling a standard setup method that you can override, and is torn down by calling teardown.

This way you can ensure that each test runs in a clean environment, so mistakes in one test don't impact another.

Most versions of the framework come with a little GUI that you can use to control which tests to run, and that shows progress and your final score. Naturally, before you release code, you run all the tests in the system, and your final score is perfect. Click one more notch forward on the progress dial.

It's tempting to use more complex testing tools. There are even some out there that claim to do intelligent "black box" testing of your classes. Read about these with some skepticism—how could they possibly know the right and wrong answers to feed to your class? They might build some skeleton methods, but that's not the important part. The important part is your application of your intelligence to testing what really needs it.

Try these xUnit tools. They're free and worth ten times that much. A hundred, maybe.

---

1. News flash! There is now www.junit.org, home for all things JUnit.

Chapter 14

Test First, by Intention

Code what you want, not how to do it. Chet and Ron do a small task test first trying always to express intention in the code rather than algorithm.

Warning: There is Smalltalk code in this example. We think you'll do fine, and ask you to try to read along. The details of the code aren't critical—the thinking and the partnering are.

Chet and I wanted to give a short demonstration to tie together all the XP programming practices. We decided to work on an actual problem that I'd encountered at a client location. This is a transcript of an actual session, not a sanitized session made up for the book. The ragged edges are real life.

There are two key things to watch for in this example. First, we write new code only when we have a test that doesn't work. We call this test-first programming.

Second, we don't think much at all about how to do a thing; we think about what we have to do. We call this programming by intention. You just write code as if someone has already written the hard method for you and you just have to send the message.

The task is this: we have two collections of Sum objects. A Sum has a name (a string) and an amount (a number). The output is to be a single collection of new Sums. If a Sum of the same name appears in each collection, the new one should have the same name and the total of their amounts. If a Sum appears in only one collection, the new one should have that amount. The order of the output should be the order of the first collection, followed by any elements from the second that didn't occur in the first (see the table that follows).

First	Second	Result
A 1	A 10	A 11
C 2	B 3	C 2
		B 3

Chet asked a few questions, mostly about whether we had any code to start with. I said that it had been ugly and didn't work, so we decided to start from scratch.

We were working on a new machine, so we started by defining a simple Sum object with a name and an amount. We didn't write tests for it because it was trivial and it was just a foil in our real example. For those who don't speak Smalltalk, we'll give a little commentary.

```
---Sum 10:25:00
```

The lines that look like the preceding one just name the class we're putting code into and the time we did it. They aren't part of Smalltalk; they're just here to give you a sense of how long things took. Here's the class definition:

```
---Sum 10:24:30
Object subclass: #Sum
instance variables: 'name amount'
```

This defines a new class named *Sum*, with instance variables *name* and *amount*. In Smalltalk, you don't have to define the types of the variables.

Now we build the Constructor Method for the class. This is a method definition. Each method definition starts with the name of the method, tabbed out one tab stop. A method definition in Smalltalk has a name that consists of one or more keywords. This one is *name:amount:*. The method definition also includes the names of the parameters. By convention, these names suggest the types of the parameters, but they are just names to be used in the code that follows.

The method itself starts on the next line, indented. So we're defining *name:amount:*. The definition is

```
^self new
    setName: aString
    amount: aNumber
```

which means (*self new*) create a new instance of this class (*Sum*), and send it the message

```
        setName: aString amount: aNumber
```

which is what we call a Constructor Parameter method. The hat character (^) means *answers*, or *returns*.

We start every class definition this same way, with a Constructor and Constructor Parameter Method. It gets you going smoothly when you always start a class the same way. Here's the whole Constructor Method:

```
---Sum class 10:25:00
name: aString amount: aNumber
    ^self new
        setName: aString
        amount: aNumber
```

The next step is always to define the Constructor Parameter method we just sent. (Smalltalk doesn't mind if you use a method before you define it, although some versions will give you a warning about it.)

```
---Sum 10:25:15
setName: aString amount: aNumber
    name := aString.
    amount := aNumber
```

This method just assigns the two parameters to the corresponding instance variables. Now the instance is initialized. We also build accessors for the instance variables because I happen to know we will need them. I was building this class from memory and was sure we'd need the accessors. It would have been better to wait to be sure.

```
---Sum 10:25:30
name
    ^name
```

This method is named *name*, and it answers (returns) the *name* instance variable. This method is an accessor for *name*. Strictly speaking we wouldn't have put this in, except that I was building this class from memory as a given.

We also built an accessor for *amount* while we were there. Bad Ron. Rolled-up newspaper for you.

```
---Sum 10:25:40
amount
    ^amount
```

OK, enough warm-up. It's time to write our object, which we have decided to call *Summarizer*. We began by making a test class named *SummarizerTest*. Here's the conversation we had as we pair programmed our way along.

CHET: What shall we test first?

RON: Let's just make an empty one. That should answer an empty collection.

Chet writes the test. He assumes that there is a method already in existence named *emptySummarizer*. This keeps him focused on the immediate task, making an empty one and making sure that its result is empty.

```
--- SummarizerTest 10:32:08
testEmpty
    | summarizer |
    summarizer := self emptySummarizer.
```

This is what we call *programming by intention*. Instead of worrying about how to create an empty Summarizer and maybe writing the code in line, Chet just expresses his intention, to have an empty Summarizer. This makes the code more clear, but more important it keeps you moving smoothly because you don't have to shift gears to think about a subordinate detail while you code the method you're on. You'll see that we do that right along.

For you non-Smalltalkers, the vertical bars set off a definition of a temporary variable named summarizer. The variable is local to the method.

Now Chet pauses before writing the first *should:* to discuss what to do.

CHET: How shall we get the answer?

RON: Let's just send *summarize* to the Summarizer.

CHET: How about *summary*?

RON: OK, that's better.

Note that here we are defining a key element of Summarizer's interface: the method you send to make it actually do its thing. To do this in a test is great because you are actually using the object, and that gives you a much better chance of defining a useful and clear interface.

```
--- SummarizerTest 10:32:08
testEmpty
    | summarizer |
    summarizer := self emptySummarizer.
    self should: [summarizer summary isEmpty]
```

The test method above just creates an *emptySummarizer* (or would if that method existed) and tests to be sure its summary is empty. Naturally, we run the test. It doesn't work, because *emptySummary* isn't defined. We expected that, but we like to run the test every chance we get—it's a good habit to have.

CHET: How do we create one of these deals?

RON: Let's define the class, give it two instance variables, call them *first* and *second*.

CHET: I hate those names.

RON: Me too, but I can't think of anything better.

```
--- Summary 10:32:45
Object subclass: #Summarizer
instance variables: 'first second'
```

We immediately go back to the test, not even making a Constructor Method because we don't know yet what we want it to look like. Looking at the blank test method for *emptySummarizer,* we discuss it:

RON: So, we need a Summarizer with two collections of Sums.

CHET: *first:second:?*

RON: How about just *with:with:?*

CHET: OK.

The name *with:with:* has good history in Smalltalk when you are creating some object with a couple of items that aren't particularly differentiated except for order. On the other hand, the name isn't very communicative. Ron may have been wrong with this suggestion.

Chet writes the method that way, putting two empty arrays into the Summarizer.

```
--- SummarizerTest 10:33:06
emptySummarizer
    ^Summarizer
        with: #()
        with: #()
```

We run the test again. It breaks, of course, because Summarizer doesn't understand the *with:with* method. Chet just types it in, along with the corresponding Constructor Parameter method. Again, it's a rote thing he just knows how to do because we always do it this way.

```
--- Summarizer class 10:35:03
with: firstCollection with: secondCollection
    ^self new
        setFirstCollection: firstCollection
        secondCollection: secondCollection

--- Summarizer 10:35:54
setFirstCollection: firstCollection secondCollection:
        secondCollection
```

```
first := firstCollection.
second := secondCollection
```

We run the test again. This time it breaks because the Summarizer doesn't understand *summary*. Chet hasn't an idea how to do the method, so he just creates one with a halt in it, then runs the test again to get into the debugger.

```
--- Summarizer 10:37:18
summary
        self halt
```

In the debugger we look around a bit.

CHET: OK, the two input collections are empty.

RON: What should we answer? I don't know what to do next.

CHET: This will work.

```
--- Summarizer 10:38:11
summary
        ^first, second
```

Chet has answered the two input collections concatenated together. I don't know why he picked this, but I can see it will work. That is, the result will be an empty collection, so the test will run. This is nearly the simplest thing that could possibly work. It would have been simpler to just answer a literal empty collection, but Chet was just getting his hands on the variables a bit.

Our first test runs. Even though the object is clearly wrong, we don't have a broken test to make us fix it. So we write another test.

RON: Let's test the example I wrote down. (The one in the table up above.)

CHET: OK.

Chet starts the method, creates a temp, and starts an assignment to it. He pauses and types a left paren. I know that he's about to try to construct the test Summarizer right there.

RON: Just send *abcSummarizer*.

CHET: Right.

RON: We have to remember to tell them how important this is.

CHET: This is one of the most important things you've taught me. I just write code that assumes that ten seconds ago someone already wrote the method I need, like the *abcSummarizer* method.

Here again, we're talking about *intention*. We just say what we want, not how to do it. When we get there, it's always easy.

```
--- SummarizerTest 10:39:34
testABC
    | summarizer |
    summarizer := self abcSummarizer.
    self should: [summarizer summary size = 3]
```

So that's what he does. Again, this is programming by intention. Chet just assumes a method *abcSummarizer* that will set up the test object. Then he writes a simple test that checks to make sure the *summary* send to this one answers back a three-element collection. It's not enough of a test, but it's enough to break, which is all we need. We go on to build the *Summarizer* to test. Note that we just copied the method—we haven't put the elements in it yet.

```
--- SummarizerTest 10:40:57
abcSummarizer
    ^Summarizer
        with: #()
        with: #()
```

Having built the *Summarizer* object, Chet was ready to enhance the test. I wasn't ready, but he was, so I rode along as he enhanced the test to check all the values.

```
--- SummarizerTest 10:43:06
testABC
    | summarizer summary |
    summarizer := self abcSummarizer.
    summary := summarizer summary.
    self should: [summary size = 3].
    self should: [summary first name = 'a'].
    self should: [summary first amount = 11].
    self should: [(summary at: 2) name = 'c'].
    self should: [(summary at: 2) amount = 2].
    self should: [summary last name = 'b'].
    self should: [summary last amount = 3].
```

RON: I guess there's no choice. We're going to have to build the collections now.

CHET: Not quite. We can still do this:

```
--- SummarizerTest 10:44:29
abcSummarizer
    ^Summarizer
        with: self acCollection
        with: self abCollection
```

Chet puts off the inevitable thinking a bit longer by declaring his intention in the method, namely to have a collection with a and c, and one with a and b. Again he assumes that a magic elf has already created them, programming his intention, not his algorithm.

Now it's pretty clear what we need since we have a name for it. So we type in the methods:

```
--- SummarizerTest 10:45:45
acCollection
    ^OrderedCollection
        with: (Sum
            name: 'a'
            amount: 1)
        with: (Sum
            name: 'c'
            amount: 2)

--- SummarizerTest 10:45:59
abCollection
    ^OrderedCollection
        with: (Sum
            name: 'a'
            amount: 10)
        with: (Sum
            name: 'b'
            amount: 3)
```

This slightly cryptic Smalltalk code just creates an *OrderedCollection* (like a Java vector) with two instances of Sum.

Great, the test is written. We run it. Oops. The original summary method that concatenates the inputs gives back four elements, not three, and the test breaks. We aren't surprised.

CHET: OK, we have to actually do summary. How?

RON: We could go over the first collection and put all of its elements into a summary collection. Then we could go over the second collection and if the element is in the summary, add it in. Otherwise, we can put it in.

CHET: That's weird. The two methods would be sort of alike, but not quite. How about if we go over each collection, and each time if the item we have is in the summary we add ours in. Otherwise, we create one?

RON: Good, I like that. So we'll just process first, and then process second.

```
--- Summarizer 10:50:29
summary
    self
        processFirst;
        processSecond
```

CHET: Where shall we put the answer?

RON: Just make a new instance variable, *summarizer*.

CHET: OK, shall I just init it in the *Constructor Parameter* method?

RON: OK.

Chet updates the class definition to add the instance variable, and the method to define it as an empty *OrderedCollection*.

```
--- Summarizer 10:51:01
setFirstCollection: firstCollection secondCollection:
    secondCollection
    first := firstCollection.
    second := secondCollection.
    summary := OrderedCollection new
```

RON: Duh. We shouldn't have two different process methods. Let's just have a *process:* method that we use twice.

CHET: Duh.

```
--- Summarizer 10:51:55
summary
    self process: first.
    self process: second
```

RON: OK, let's write *process:*.

Chet writes a loop over the collection, pausing for a moment to think how to process the items. Then he remembers to just declare his intention (*processItem:*) and go on.

```
--- Summarizer 10:52:32
process: aCollection
    aCollection do: [:each | self processItem: each]
```

Collections in Smalltalk know how to iterate themselves. The above code sends *processItem:* to each object in the input collection *aCollection*.

It's getting close now. We run the test and notice we don't have *processItem:* defined yet. Chet makes a blank method, then we talk.

```
--- Summarizer 10:52:42
processItem: aSum
```

RON: OK, rubber meeting road here. What shall we do?

CHET: Well, we just find the matching Sum in the summary.

RON: And add our input Sum into it! Do it!

```
--- Summarizer 10:54:22
processItem: aSum
    (self matchingSum: aSum) add: aSum
```

Chet codes just what we said. Our intention is to find matching Sum, add our input Sum into it. The code says just that. Now we run the test and, of course, *matchingSum* isn't defined.

RON: We have to go through the existing summary items and see if we have a matching one—

CHET: *Detect*!

RON: Yes, do a *detect*—

CHET: And *ifAbsent:*

RON: *ifNone:*

CHET: I can never remember which it is.

RON: Make a new *Sum* and put it in the *summary.*

Chet codes it up. This is standard Smalltalk idiom, so he codes the whole thing in line. The code just says that it'll find a Sum in the summary with matching name if there is one; if not it'll create a new one of that name, and put it in. In either case, it gives back the new or existing matching Sum. You could make a case that we should have broken it up, but we discussed it and couldn't find a way we liked better.

```
--- Summarizer 10:56:40
matchingSum: aSum
    ^summary
        detect: [:each | each name = aSum name]
        ifNone: [summary add: (Sum
            name: aSum name
            amount: 0)]
```

We run the test. It doesn't run because *Sum* doesn't understand how to add. We quickly build that.

```
--- Sum 10:58:40
add: aSum
    amount := amount + aSum amount
```

We run the test again. It doesn't work. Instead of getting a collection of *Sums* back, we get back the *Summarizer*. This means we forgot to answer back the result. I recognize this immediately.

RON: Jeffries error type 1. We didn't answer the collection. Where was my partner?

CHET: Driving. You were supposed to help *me*.

RON: Oh.

```
--- Summarizer
10:59:31
summary
    self process: first.
    self process: second.
    ^summary
```

We add the final line to *summary*, then run the test. It runs. We celebrate briefly, wishing we had a bell to ring. Then we begin to review the code now that it works, to see if we should clean it up.

CHET: *process:* isn't a very good name.

RON: We could say *summarize:*.

CHET: OK.

```
--- Summarizer 11:04:45
summary
    self summarize: first.
    self summarize: second.
    ^summary
```

Chet runs the test. It breaks, there's no *summarize:* method. He renames the *process:* method.

```
--- Summarizer 11:04:53
summarize: aCollection
    aCollection do: [:each | self processItem: each]
```

Chet runs the test and it works. But he doesn't like the new method the way it is.

CHET: Oops, better change *processItem:* to *summarizeItem:* while we're at it.

RON: Good.

He changes *summarize:* to send *summarizeItem:*.

```
--- Summarizer 11:05:30
summarize: aCollection
    aCollection do: [:each | self summarizeItem: each]
```

Running the test, Chet "discovers" that *summarizeItem:* isn't defined, and renames *processItem:* to *summarizeItem:*.

```
--- Summarizer 11:05:42
summarizeItem: aSum
    (self matchingSum: aSum) add: aSum
```

The test runs again. At this point we look at what we have done and find it good. We stop, and go to lunch at Red Hot and Blue. We each have a Pulled Pig sandwich.

Review Remarks

An online reviewer, Jim, remarks:

Well, "summarize" and "summarizeItem" were fairly simple one-liners. Not much to break there. But "matchingSum" was longer and possibly worth testing, at least to my non-Smalltalk trained eyes. Perhaps an experienced Smalltalker would disagree and say that "matchingSum" was obviously correct.

I think Jim is probably right. When we wrote the method, it just flowed out in good Smalltalk style. But as I mentioned above, Chet and I looked hard at it, hoping to make it more clear. We couldn't think of anything, and it was working fine, so we stopped.

On another day, I might experiment with breaking out the lookup aspect of the object. It kind of seems like overkill, but there's a common behavior one uses a lot that might be called *Lookup Matching* or *Add One* of These. We might discover a useful object someday if we play with that.

The bottom line is always judgment. If the code's not clear enough, it needs more work and probably more tests. Jim was right to wonder.

A triumph of Internet-based collective code ownership. Thanks, Jim!

Summary

Experiment with writing little tests first, and with always expressing your intention, not algorithm, in the code you write. We think you'll find that the work goes more smoothly, and you wind up with code that communicates its meaning clearly.

Chapter 15

Releasing Changes

Using collective code ownership and comprehensive unit tests, an
XP team releases changes rapidly and reliably.

An XP team practices collective code ownership: every class and method belongs to the team, and any team member can improve anything that needs it. Collective code ownership lets the team make faster progress because no one has to wait until someone else gets around to fixing something. The code stays cleaner because programmers aren't forced to work around a deficiency in one object by hacking up another.

One of the most important parts of making collective code ownership work is the process of releasing changes to other programmers on the team. This chapter won't tell you everything you need to know about code management, but it will give you some ideas about how to interact with your code manager.

When an XP programming pair is working, their code goes through three phases. These phases are

1. Local. This is the first phase of development. The pair has just started working, and their changes are not available to any of the other developers.
2. Release candidate. The programmers have finished their task, and are ready to begin the process of releasing their changes to the other programmers.
3. Released to the repository. This is the current official version of the code. This code is guaranteed to work. That is, all of the unit tests run at 100 percent. Released changes are available to all of the other programmers.

Throughout the day, an XP programming pair would probably release changes at least once and potentially many more times. Meanwhile, other pairs have also been making changes and releasing them, and there's a chance they will have changed the same things you did. You'll need an approach to releasing your changes that keeps things running smoothly.

The process we recommend goes like this:

1. Always start with all of the released code. This ensures that you are starting with the latest and best versions of everything.
2. Write tests that correspond to your task. (Write the test first.)
3. Run all the unit tests.

4. Fix any unit tests that are broken. Since you started with the released code, the only tests that should break are the ones you just wrote. It is your responsibility to fix them.

5. When all of the unit tests run at 100 percent, your local changes become release candidates.

6. Release candidate changes are integrated with the currently released code. We recommend the use of a separate integration machine for this, and we'll describe it that way. Go to the integration machine. Load all the released code. Load all of your release candidate changes. Then check for conflicting edits. The currently released code should be the same code you started from. If it isn't, another pair has released before you. This doesn't happen often, but let's assume that it has.

7. If the released code was modified while you were making your changes, compare the differences between your changes and the released code. Use a diff tool if possible, not just your eyes. Identify the changes released by the other pair(s), and integrate those changes with your changes. Ask the other pair for help if you need it.

8. Once you have integrated any necessary changes, run the unit tests on the integration machine. They should run to 100 percent, and they usually will. If they don't, it usually means you've missed integrating something, or that your changes and someone else's conflict. The unit tests that fail will pinpoint the problem. Fix all the problems. Again, get help from the other pairs if you need it.

9. When the unit tests run at 100 percent, release all of your code—that is, make the code on the integration machine the official version.

The release process generally goes more quickly than it took to write about it. A few minutes to load your release candidates on the integration machine, a quick check for conflicting edits, ten minutes to run the unit tests, and then the code can be marked as released.

Code Management Tools

The code management tool used on your project can make a huge difference in your productivity. Ideally, whatever tool you use, it should make it easy to do the following tasks:

1. Identify local changes
2. Differentiate between local changes and released code

3. Identify who released a change, and when they released it
4. Merge changes and released code
5. Revert to previously released code

If you're using VA Smalltalk, VW Smalltalk, or VA Java, we recommend using ENVY. There are alternatives, but ENVY is the preferred choice in our opinion.

In other environments, or if you just can't swing the price, a tool like CVS, Visual SourceSafe, PVCS, MKS, or TLIB will do the job. There are lots of code managment tools out there—read this chapter, then check them out and pick one.

In general, set as few restrictions as possible into the code management tool. No passwords, no group restrictions, as little ownership hassle as possible. Your objective is for everyone to own everything. Everyone has equal rights to all code.

Begin your project with no segmentation into code groups or topics. It's best to use a flat structure as long as possible. Let the flow of code development tell you what organization is needed, when the time comes. Then refactor the code database.

Troubleshooting

The two most common problems with releasing changes are slow merges due to conflicting edits, and lost changes.

Slow Merges

Occasional conflicting edits are a natural result of going rapidly with collective ownership. In the beginning of your project they will be more common; if you only have one class, everyone is going to be making changes to it. As your system grows, conflicting edits should become fewer and fewer. If this is not the case, the best way to solve this problem is to release your changes more frequently. This will reduce the likelihood that two pairs will conflict. See *Continuous Integration* (page 78)

Some teams try to avoid simultaneously editing anything. Please don't do this—moving where the code leads is more important than the occasional collision of conflicting edits. Instead, edit what needs it, and deal with collisions as they happen.

- -

In rare cases, you may need a more formal check-out/check-in process for a few classes. Avoid this if you can, but be alert for the need to do it if too much time is spent merging changes.

Also be aware that different classes will become *hot*. It might be a good idea to sign up for tasks with hot classes in mind, so that fewer pairs will be likely to need the same classes.

Lost Changes

Lost changes are a nuisance and a waste of time. The main cause of lost changes is incorrectly merging release candidate changes with released code. This is usually because a conflicting edit was not recognized, or the programmer incorrectly merged the two sets of changes.

The solution to this problem has three parts. The first two parts of the solution are always start with all of the released code and always release changes frequently. Frequent releases minimize the chance that the released code has changed. When changes do have to be merged, frequent releases minimize the impact. Remember *Continuous Integration* (page 78).

The third part of the solution is your *Unit Tests* (page 93). Code can't stay lost for long if there's a test somewhere relying on it. Be sure you add tests whenever you add code to any class. Since all the unit tests must all run at 100 percent before any code is released, this ensures that other programmers can't break your code by accident.

Another common cause of lost changes is intentional reversion. Sometimes you want to roll a class back to a previously released version. When this is done, you will of course lose all the changes relating to that path. Unfortunately, you will also lose valid changes that were done along the way. The solution for this type of lost change is to go forward, not back. Start with the currently released code, and identify the differences between it and the desired version. Then edit the currently released code to bring it back into line with the previously released version, but retaining any new code. These changes are release candidates, and when the unit tests all run at 100 percent, the code can be released.

Finally, back up your source code. An XP project is like any other in this regard: you can be sure you'll lose the source manager files as soon as they aren't backed up. So use normal precautions in setting up procedures for use of the tool you choose.

Conclusion

Code management and your release process are right when they are unobtrusive. It should be easy and fast to get the source you need. It should be easy and fast to save your changes. The code manager should detect conflicts, and resolving them should be straightforward. There should be no waiting—if a pair needs to edit something, they should feel free to go ahead.

A good Extreme pair saves code very frequently, many times per day. If the code manager is making you want to release less often, fix the code manager. Rapid progress depends on rapid and frequent release.

Chapter 16

Do or Do Not

We've now covered most of the programming aspects of XP.
Here's a summary of things we do—and things we don't do.

Extreme Programming is about doing. For each key aspect of software development, XP prescribes a few simple practices aimed at helping you know when you are done and know when you are right.

But XP is also about not doing. Over the years, software development methodology has become encrusted with practices that, for most projects, do not advance the actual effort of producing the product that is wanted: the software.

The result of an XP project should be a computer program. Not just any computer program, but a well-crafted, flexibly structured, properly documented computer program, shown by testing to meet known and documented requirements.

Remember that if you're doing XP right, at the end of the project you will have a computer program that is

❖ well designed
❖ well crafted
❖ flexibly structured
❖ properly documented
❖ tested
❖ meeting known and documented requirements

Some of the things that we advise against doing are a bit controversial. As you review the simple XP processes, we're sure you'll see that the other things aren't always necessary after all. Use your own best judgment.

Here are some recommendations:

❖ Don't try to design the whole system before you start implementing it. Usually requirements changes alone will make this impossible. In any case, no existing design methodology is effective enough to prevent problems during implementation, and a process of design a little, build a little will allow you to learn faster and get a quality system done sooner.
❖ Do design all the time. Begin simply, and as you learn what the design should be, refactor to make it so. Never stop designing, never stop making the code agree with what the design should be.
❖ Don't try to freeze requirements before you start implementing. Requirements changes show that the customer is learning! Sure, it would be nice if they knew just what they wanted before you

started building things, but the fact is that when they see what you're building, they'll learn what they meant. XP lets you use a development and planning approach that allows for change, without a big up-front investment in frameworks or flexibility.

✧ Do get comfortable with taking on any story in any order. Sure, sometimes order makes a difference, but more often than we programmers think, it doesn't. Just tell the customers the cost of every story, and let them choose.

✧ Don't produce voluminous design documents at the beginning. Don't even produce them in the middle: produce them at the end, when you actually know something. Extreme Programming teaches you how to keep the design flexible, for rapid change and fastest implementation. The design documents you produce at the beginning will go out of date very quickly (they always do, even on non-Extreme projects), and you'll either waste time updating the docs or let them get out-of-date. Either is bad.

✧ Do focus on communication. A few diagrams can help. A big picture on the wall can help. More important, however, are clear code and talking, talking, talking.

✧ Don't produce documents or other artifacts that aren't being used. If you couldn't resist writing up the design or drawing some UML, notice whether anyone is really using the documents. If they aren't, stop producing them. For extra credit, erase the ones you have already created—they're out of date anyway, aren't they?

✧ Do pay attention to your metrics and your key reporting graphs. The project's progress needs to be published frequently. Most of the design probably does not.

✧ Don't separate the team into designers and coders. Let everyone reach their own level in design and coding.

✧ Do let everyone get involved in design. Do group design, using CRC, for everything important. This will let everyone learn and participate. And let's face it, the most junior person on the team is as likely as anyone to spot a design flaw.

✧ Don't build for tomorrow. When you hear yourself elaborating or generalizing a design, stop. Implement the simplest design that could possibly work to do what you have to do right now. When you say, "We're gonna need," you're wasting precious time, and you're usurping the customer's right to set priorities.

- ✦ Don't build for tomorrow. When you read the preceding paragraph, you may have said, "But it'll be harder to put it in later." That turns out to be incorrect almost every time. If you leave the code simple and true today, improving it tomorrow will be easy. And you'll be smarter tomorrow: you'll know more about what is really needed, and you'll know more about how to do things.

- ✦ Do build cleanly for today. Do the simple thing that solves today's problem, but do it well. Keep the code of high quality, just right for today's needs.

- ✦ Don't build for tomorrow. OK, we know that you're good enough to look to the future. But XP is a team discipline, and everyone has to play by the same rules. Look around the room. Probably you see someone who shouldn't be building for the future, because they'll get it wrong or make it too elaborate. In fairness to them, you're going to give up building for tomorrow, so that they'll give it up as well. (And just ignore all those people looking at you while they read this paragraph.)

Chapter 17

Experience
Improves Estimates

With each iteration, we gain experience. Experience with stories helps us estimate future stories more easily and more accurately.

You've just released your changes for some task. When you finish all the tasks in a story, it's time to take a moment. For example, when Chet and I wrote the Summarizer program in *Test First, by Intention* (page 107), it took us about an hour. From now on, we'll have a good idea of how long it takes to do tasks that are about that hard. And of course it's not difficult to estimate whether a given task is about the same size as the Summarizer, or half as big or twice as big.

This means that when we have a task like that one, we can estimate about how long it will take and be pretty reliable. And the more we estimate, and the more we pay attention to how things really turn out, the better we'll do.

Some tasks, of course, aren't anything at all like the Summarizer. That's fine, you have lots of tasks and lots of time. As you do your first few tasks interfacing with the database, note how long they take. As you write the first couple of reports, note how long they take. And so on.

You can read more about task creation in *Team Brainstorms Engineering Tasks* (page 63), and in *How to Estimate Anything* (page 185), but the simple answer is that when the team has a big thing to do, team members brainstorm how to break it down, until it is broken into small enough tasks that experience allows them to estimate.

The important things to remember about XP task estimation are just these:

1. Estimate each task that you sign up for. Don't try to get down to minutes—it's probably best in a project not to go below half a day. For the Summarizer, I estimated two hours, but it took only one. My partner was great.

2. Estimate the amount of actual time you will spend working, with a partner, at the machine, on the task. Don't worry about time you'll spend discussing it, drawing pictures, or thinking. These things will all average out when you measure your velocity. The important thing is the size of the solution, in time spent implementing.

3. Pay attention to the actual time you spend working, at the machine, on the task. You can write it on a card if you want to, but since you'll usually focus on just one task at a time, memory will probably suffice.

4. Take a moment. You estimated a day. It took a day and a half. Or you estimated a day and it took only a half a day. What was it that you missed in the estimate that would help you estimate better next time?

It should be pretty clear that if you do this a lot, you'll get really good at estimating how long things will take. Feeding this knowledge back into each iteration plan makes things go more and more smoothly and easily.

Chapter 18

Resources, Scope, Quality, Time

Who's doing what? How much is finished? How good is it? When will we be done? What metrics should we keep?

It's important to know where we are, whether we are programmers, customers, or managers. We have to know because we want to be sure we're doing well.

Even if things aren't going according to plan, everyone needs to know. It's tempting to sugarcoat things, but everyone has the right to the truth.

XP prescribes tracking and reporting approaches that are easy and public. This ensures that everyone's always on the same page. Briefly, it goes like this:

Resources

Keep track of key resources: planned versus actual; number of developers; number of customers assigned to the project; number of testers; number of computers in development, test, production; and so on.

Scope

Keep track of the number of stories over time: how many exist; how many are done; how many more are expected. Consider tracking total estimated time for the project and estimated versus actual scope consumption.

Quality

Use a standard acceptance testing graph showing number of tests and number succeeding over time.

Time

Track the results of each release plan. Graph schedule versus time. Discuss dropped or added functionality and its impact on time.

Tracking and Reporting Scope

Kent Beck says you should report scope by picking up the stack of story cards and saying, "This is everything we have to do." Then you divide the cards into two stacks and say, "This is what we have done so far, and this is what we have left to do," showing the two stacks.

As a first approximation, this is just about right. You probably need to track the history of progress, and your management might be comfortable with just a bit more information.

Here are a few graphs. Pick the simplest one that could possibly work in your situation. Don't move up the scale of complexity unless your experience on the current project says you have to.

For each iteration, graph how many story cards exist and how many are done, on a bar chart (see Figure 18.1). Color completed cards green and those still to be done white. (Not red—red means bad. We'll use black and white here.)

Take a look at this graph. What is it telling us? The growing portion of black shows that we're making good progress. But we seem to be getting more stories as well. What's up with that?

It's your project, so you'd better know. Here are some possibilities:

❖ Stories are being split for better planning (release plan). In this case the work isn't really increasing, and everything is probably OK. Consider adjusting the historical columns to show the new story count also.

❖ Stories are being added because progress is good. This can actually happen and, if you can make the original date, might be OK. Consider scheduling an early release with the original stories, followed by another quick release with the new ones. Consider showing the new stories as a yellow section of the bar.

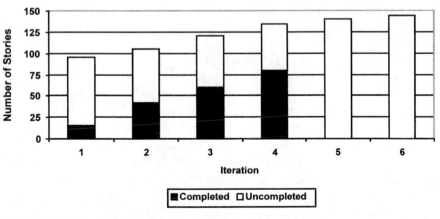

FIGURE 18.1 Completed stories

❖ Stories are being added and the date is in jeopardy. This is "scope creep," and generally it is bad. People will remember that you were late, and not that you did more. Use the planning process to reduce scope to hit your promised date, and then do a quick second release.

I may seem fanatical about making the date. If I am, it's because many years of development tell me that the date is what management remembers. XP lets you predict your progress accurately, and manage scope to make that date. For my money, that's the most impressive thing your team can do.

Now unless you dozed off, you probably want to object that just counting the cards loses the fact that some stories are big and some are small. That's true, yet it probably doesn't matter. Since you're doing the worst things first, if anything you should speed up toward the end as you get into all that easy stuff.

But if it really matters to you, use the same graph but show estimated weeks of work (Gummi Bears, points, or XPUs) instead of card count. Each time you do a new release plan, use the new numbers in all the subsequent graph columns. There's probably no need to do anything to the historical columns.

Frankly, the effort graph is probably overkill. The charts aren't that different, and the second one is much more hassle to create. If you just draw the standard scope graph after each iteration, you'll know and express more about your progress than most projects ever do.

Go for it!

Tracking and Reporting Quality

OK, the first and most important quality graph is unit test scores over time. Here it is (see Figure 18.2). Copy it out of the book and post it on the wall.

That's right. You must have unit tests for everything that could possibly break, and they must always be at 100 percent, for every release of code by every programmer. That's one graph done.

The official public XP measure of quality is, of course, your acceptance tests. What are the most important dimensions of acceptance tests?

The number of acceptance tests gives a good measure of the scope of your testing. And the number of tests succeeding tells you how well you're doing.

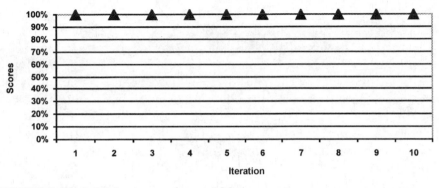

Unit Test Scores

FIGURE 18.2 Unit tests—always 100 percent

What should the graph of number of acceptance tests look like? As you get close to release, it should flatten out, as you think of fewer and fewer things that still need testing. It will probably start slowly and ramp up, giving a classic S-curve (see Figure 18.3).

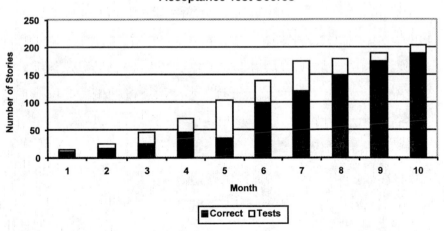

Acceptance Test Scores

■ Correct □ Tests

FIGURE 18.3 Acceptance tests

The success curve will generally be lower than the number of tests. Yes, if your code is perfect and never breaks, they'll be equal. If you can really do that, go for it, and write and tell us how. For the rest of us, we'll color under the graph, green for success and red for failure. Put the green on the bottom since it shows progress better. In this book we'll use white and black.

Graph the scores at the end of every iteration, for a graph like the one above. Within the team, you'll want to graph the scores more frequently, preferably every day (see Figure 18.4).

For your monthly report, these graphs will probably suffice to show progress toward quality at completion. Internally, however, you may want more.

Usually your acceptance tests will break out into some natural organization. Each of these breakouts will probably have several, perhaps many individual tests in it. If you want to see how errors are clumping by product area, produce a graph showing success/failure by area (see Figure 18.5).

It's probably sufficient to show product area graphs scaled to 100 percent. If your groups vary a lot in number of tests, you'll probably have to scale them. If they're all about the same size anyway, you could show them at natural scale; if they're all about the same size, there's no

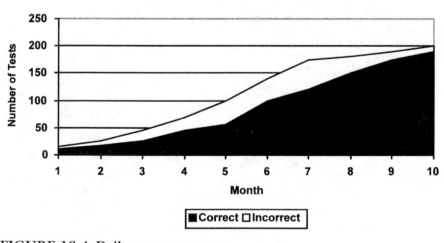

FIGURE 18.4 Daily acceptance tests

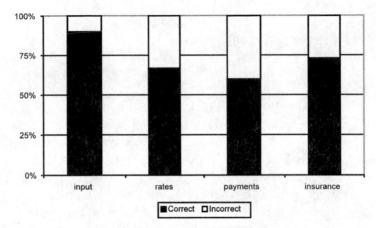

FIGURE 18.5 Acceptance test scores by product area

real benefit to doing so. Try the charts both ways and use the ones you prefer.

The point of this graph is to identify, daily, things that are improving or breaking (see Figure 18.6). Compare this chart with the previous one.

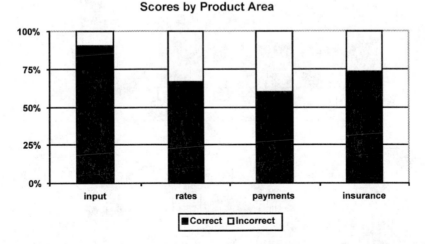

FIGURE 18.6 Acceptance test scores by product area—changed!

What happened? A bunch of the payment group's tests broke. They need attention—we may need to beef up the unit tests for some part of the code because there's definitely a bug that slipped through somewhere.

Another useful graph, especially as you near perfection and release, is the up or down change in the number of successful tests (see Figure 18.7).

Take a look at that big dip. A bunch of tests broke that day. The next day a few came back, and over the next couple of days it looks as if they all came back. You can tell a lot about what's going on in the system from a simple chart like this.

Set up your acceptance testing process to produce a few numbers each day, and enter them into Excel or your favorite spreadsheet. Run the graphs and put them on the wall. Talk about them at the daily stand-up meeting. Your tester should bring up the test topic every day even if nothing changed: "Running acceptance tests. Numbers 3701 and 4130 are still bad. A couple of others broke, but Susan says she knows what happened and they'll be fixed by tonight."

Here's an acceptance test chart that is hard to draw by machine, but easy to do by hand. It shows an empty box for an existing test that's running wrong, and a full box if it's running right (see Figure 18.8).

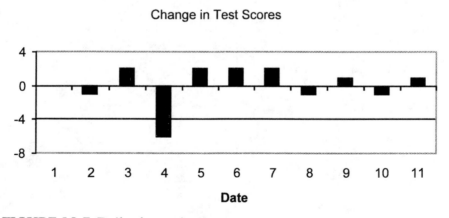

FIGURE 18.7 Daily change in test scores

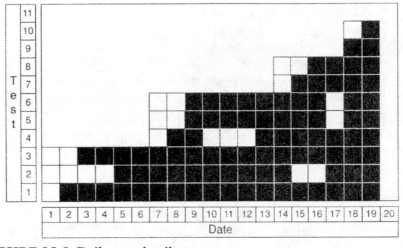

FIGURE 18.8 Daily test detail

When we look at this chart, we see blocks of tests coming on line. It takes a day or so before they run right, but then they usually continue to run right along. But something happened to test four on the 10th, to test two on the 15th, and to tests five and six on the 17th.

When it's time for your status report, even if it's to the president, take the test charts off the wall and show him. If you just have to make slides, I suppose it's OK to print them from the spreadsheet. But be certain you are reporting the same data you look at every day. Good or bad, that's the Extreme way: tell the truth straight out.

What About Other Metrics?

There are many interesting metrics, and most of them are easy to track. The number of classes, number of methods, and number of methods per class are all kept historically of course. Other metrics are source lines, story completion rate, tasks per story, and pair programming time versus reported defect rate.

There are lots of great metrics. Color charts and rates of change. Fantastic, and with a few scripts, a little Perl, some Excel, you could know so much.

Stop! Cut it out! Don't do that!

The success of your project is measured in Resources, Scope, Quality, and Time. Track these, as shown here, and you'll know more about your project than most teams ever do.

The success of your project is in your people. Watch these few variables, and if they show there's trouble, talk to the people. Watch the people. Are people relaxed, friendly, playing around, and throwing Nerf balls at each other? Good. Are their heads down, avoiding eye contact, and snapping at each other? Not good.

Watch the people. You can spot trouble coming and avert it long before it will ever show up in your metrics.

You Can't Resist, Can You?

OK, you can't resist some metrics, and you might want to write up your project for the journals.

So keep a daily journal. The real metrics are the things that happen in the real world. Write in your journal every day at a fixed time, recording the events of the previous 24 hours. Evening is probably best for memory, if it works for you.

Here are some things Ron has been asked, or asked himself, that he sometimes wishes he had written down:

- ✧ Number of classes and methods by date
- ✧ Number of test classes, methods, and asserts by date
- ✧ Number of stories available by date
- ✧ Number of stories replaced, destroyed, split by date
- ✧ Risks identified
- ✧ Daily journal of feelings and observations
- ✧ Significant events or comments made by people

But here's the telling thing: while a number of these items would be interesting in papers or in conversations at conferences, not one of them would have helped the project succeed even a little bit better. Sure, we can see how they *might* have helped. But the chances of their helping are awfully small. They're not worth taking time away from actually working.

Facts are your best friend, even if they aren't in your favor. But if you track them, the facts probably will be in your favor! At the end of the project, you may want to have a retrospective, to help the organization learn. When you do, it can be difficult to reconstruct certain bits of history.

- ✧ What was the project velocity in terms of stories per unit of time? Alternatively, what was the load factor, and how has it changed?
- ✧ What was the schedule and number of completed points you predicted at each release plan?
- ✧ How did the acceptance test scores change over time?
- ✧ How rapidly did the code turn over? Did you get more or less reuse within the system than you expected?

So you must either accept that there will be varying recollections of some of these things, or you must record some minimum amount of historical information somewhere.

In the end, you must use your own judgment on what to record. But please, don't be a manager who fiddles with his spreadsheet while the project burns. Success is in your people—work with them.

Chapter 19

Steering

The estimates are wrong. Your priorities will change. You must steer.

STEER

You're smart people, and you're going to be learning during the course of your project. Customers will learn what they want by seeing what they get and by learning the cost of the features they would like to have. The programmers will learn that some things are harder than they thought, and that some things are easier. They will learn good ways of doing work that they need to do a lot of, and they'll build tools to make things go faster.

The results of this are clear. I'm sure your own history will agree when you look back on it: on most projects, the estimates are often wrong, far too high or far too low, and the priorities will change before you even begin, let alone before you get to the end.

XP's practices help with the estimates. Many of the estimates you've heard about, where projects took far longer than they were "supposed" to, were based on demands, not on measured performance and estimates of difficulty. So the estimates of an XP team tend to be quite good. However, there will still be variability. You will inevitably find, over the course of the project, that a large number of stories become easier and easier to do. Most teams find that there are stories where the first couple take a few days each, and the remaining similar ones can be done at ten per day.

Most teams also find that there are some stories that take much longer than originally estimated. It's easy to be upset by this or to look for someone to blame. (Look no further: *It's Chet's Fault*, page 193.) Software is difficult. Specifying software is difficult, and building it is difficult. There's no need to make it more difficult, so let's not. Instead, let's just assess our situation and steer the project on to success.

When things take longer than they should, take that result into account in your planning. Fact is, "we'll make it up later" rarely happens, and it's not the way to bet. If you are the fortunate project that hits the Making It Up Later lottery, don't worry, you'll have plenty of ideas about what to do with the extra time. Consider selling it to all the projects that don't hit the lottery. Or use it to put additional value into your project.

Plan to proceed at the pace you're measuring. If certain stories are going slowly, look for similar ones and assume that they will go slowly as well. Get the team to reestimate those stories, or, for that matter, all stories. Use that information to decide which stories to do first, and which to defer. If it looks as if some important story that you were putting off won't get done, move it forward, at the expense of things that don't look so important now.

Steering your project will give you great pleasure and great success. As you learn what you need, an XP team can adapt to those needs. As you learn how long things take, you can rearrange stories and split stories to build an excellent product. Frankly, we believe that the process of selecting and steering will deliver a better product than getting everything you originally imagine you'll want. And the most important thing is, steering to success is actually possible.

Chapter 20

Steering the Iteration

To steer each iteration, you need to track how many stories are getting done and how well the task estimates are holding up.

When we planned the iteration, we broke the stories down into tasks, then signed up and estimated in terms of days of work.

Get Stories Done

The main point of each iteration is to complete stories. If the customer brings ten stories, and the programmers brainstorm ten tasks for each story, what should they do if they're only able to complete 90 of those 100 tasks? One possible thing would be to get each of the ten stories 90 percent done. We think that's not going to impress the customer. In fact, we hereby instruct the customer: accept only real completion on your stories. Ten stories 90 percent done equals zero stories done.

A better way would be to get nine of the stories completely done and skip one—the least valuable one. Nine stories 100 percent done plus one story zero percent done equals nine stories done. Much better than zero.

Improve Estimates

Story delivery is important, but it's not the only thing. Since we base all our planning on estimated difficulty, we need to get feedback on difficulty. When we planned the iteration, we broke each story into tasks, and the programmer who signed up estimated each task. During the iteration, we need to reflect on these estimates.

First of all, if an estimate is turning out to be seriously wrong, it could jeopardize finishing the story, so we want to check up on how we're doing against estimates frequently enough to let us reallocate resources to get things done. Second, reflecting on how long tasks take will help you estimate better next time.

Experience in task estimation, with feedback, will improve the programmers' ability to estimate. This will feed back into the estimation of stories that you do during the release plan. With improved estimation at the story level, you'll have improved information about what you can accomplish and when. This increases the chance of project success.

Tracking

If the main point of the iteration is to get stories done, then the main purpose of steering the iteration is to make that happen. All during the iteration, we want to steer so as to make sure that as many stories as possible get completed. To accomplish that, we need to track the tasks. Sometimes, we call the person with this responsibility the tracker.

The team needs to check, every few days, how all the tasks are going. You can do this by having the tracker go around to all the programmers every few days or by covering task progress at the morning stand-up. Having someone make the rounds is better if you can find someone who can do it without driving everyone mad—do you hear me—mad.

Sometimes a programmer will go off track. She may make the wrong choice at some decision point or make a poor choice of where to begin. Often programmers feel that they are "just about" to solve the problem—they can be just about to crack it for days at a time. Tracking is an independent check of how things are going. The tracking function identifies tasks that are going beyond their estimates and gives the team a chance to deal with them. More tasks get completed this way, and the team is more successful and confident.

All you need to do tracking is the contents of the iteration plan: the stories chosen, the tasks to be done, who signed up, and what their estimate was. Oh, and you need the programmers, so you can talk to them.

You need a pencil or pen along with some cards, a clipboard, or a spiral notebook. Some people record tracking results in a spreadsheet, and tracking products are coming on the market. But the essence of tracking is the face-to-face contact and a couple of numbers per task. Paper works fine.

It's tempting to "just have the programmers e-mail in their results every couple of days." Forget it. XP is about people, not computers. Eye contact is important. The team-building human contact is important.

We'll pretend you're using cards. If you're not, make suitable adjustments to what we say here. Write each programmer's name at the top of a card. On the card, write each task he signed up for, plus his initial estimate. Leave a little space between tasks. But don't worry, since you can make a new card if you mess this one up.

Talk to each programmer like this:

"Hi Dave, I'm here to track. You signed up for task XYZ. How much time have you worked on it so far?"

Dave replies, "About a day."

Then ask, "How much do you think you have to go?"

"About one more day."

"You initially estimated two days. So it's going about as you thought?"

"Yes, it's going fine."

"Dave, you also signed up for ABC. How much time on that so far?"

"Well, I've got two days in on that, and I think maybe about a day to go."

Your ears prick up. (If you can actually do this, you are a born tracker.)
"You originally estimated a day and a half. What happened?"

"Well, it's taking longer than I thought."

From Dave's vagueness, you get that the ABC task is in trouble. You may ask more questions, might suggest a CRC session, or might ask the coach to drop in on Dave and his partner. It's not Dave's fault; these things happen. The thing to do is to make sure that it gets sorted out.

Here are steps to initiate when you discover that the iteration is off track.

First of all, bring the information to the team level. A story not getting done is not an individual's problem; it is the team's problem. The sooner you start moving on it, the better you'll perform. See *It's Chet's Fault* on page 193 for one way of dealing with the blame aspect. Coach Dave to bring it up himself, or offer to handle it for him. Don't let it slide.

Second, solve the story problem within the programming team, if possible. Often other people are ahead of schedule or can buckle down a little bit to pick up the slack to complete all stories. If this can be done, it should be done. The programmers should make it be a point of honor that the team makes commitments whenever possible.

Third, give some special attention to the particular task that's off track. Call a *Quick Design Session* (page 69), in almost every case, to make sure the best minds are looking at what has turned out to be a problem task. Consider giving the task owner a new partner or even switching owners. Sometimes you're just down a rat hole on a task and a new pair will do better. Yes, we know that will feel like a defeat, but move to another task and play that one to win. The iteration is the important thing.

Fourth, if the team just can't pick up the slack, get the customer involved. Level with the customer about what's happening, and ask what to do. Sometimes they'll have you drop a story—and often it's a different one from what you expect. Sometimes they'll simplify a story, so that all stories can be completed, but one is a bit smaller than first planned. In any case, it's the customer's call. Strange as it may seem, you'll engender more confidence by getting them involved as soon as there's trouble. And confidence is what will get you a successful release.

The Benefits of Tracking

We do recommend that teams have a tracker. However, every team we've worked with has had trouble getting someone to fit the position. The tracker needs to have a nonthreatening approach to getting information, needs to be sensitive to body language and other nonverbal behavior, and needs to be willing and able to track on a regular basis.

We've tried it with peers, customers, managers, and people who happened by on the street. Our best experience was with a manager who was really good at being nonjudgmental, but whose slightly sad expression when people fell short encouraged them to do their best for him. Our worst experience was when we tried switching to a different tracker each iteration, making it a rotating duty among the programmers. The individual variability in personality and style just didn't help.

A close second in undesirability, by the way, is using the customer for tracking. It's difficult for the customer to be nonjudgmental, as she is rightly so involved in getting the most done. And the customer is prone to solve the problem on the spot instead of letting the team solve those that they can.

Tracking is a critical activity, giving you the best chance of recovering from stumbles within the iteration, helping with the ongoing communication in the team, and adding confidence. It helps you be sure you deliver complete stories rather than stories that are "nearly done." It helps programmers focus a bit on their estimates, improving your ability to know what's going to happen. Finally, it puts a little attention on the task brainstorming process, by finding those cases where the task list wasn't complete and by helping the team learn from the mistake.

You can track with a tracker, if you can find one. You can track during your daily stand-up meetings. There are probably other ways, as well. One way or another, track the iteration as it goes along. Steering is best if you do it all the time.

Chapter 21

Steering
the Release

To steer the release, you need to track what's done, how fast you are going, and how well the system works.

At the release level, there are only a couple of interesting things to know: when are you going to release, and what will you have when you do so.

Often you have a specified date by which you are supposed to release your product. By controlling scope, you can steer your project to release the best possible product by that day.

Sometimes, you have a minimal level of capability that really must be there before you release. Even in these cases, you can usually release earlier by judiciously controlling the scope, but there is some absolute minimum below which you just can't go.

This chapter is about counting what's done, so the first thing is to know what's done. That's the role of your acceptance tests. Review *Resources, Scope, Quality, Time* (page 135) and use some of those graphs, every day, to be sure done means done.

A release consists of a selection of stories implemented in the system. To know how close you are to release, you just need to know which stories are finished and which remain to be done. Finished, of course, means that the code is in the system and that it runs correctly, passing its acceptance tests. Here's a simple chart:

```
Points Done: xxxxxxxx
Proj Points: xxxxxxxxxxxxxxxxxxxxxxxxxxxxxxxx
```

Look, one-fourth done! Could it be that easy? To a first, but very good approximation, the answer is yes. Here's why:

Programmers can easily estimate comparative difficulty. And as the project goes on, their estimates will improve. And, as the project goes on, the speed at which the team implements things will be fairly stable. If it takes a programmer two weeks to implement a one-point story in this iteration, it'll probably be about two weeks for other one-point stories later on. That gives us the basic tracking item: the number of story points implemented in every iteration. Whether you use ideal programming time or Gummi Bears, just count them.

The number of points per iteration will probably be pretty stable from one to the next. It'll go down if a lot of people are on vacation, get distracted by a course, go to a planning meeting, or have lots of support requirements. It'll go up, too, especially as the team learns how to do things or builds new tools. Factoring out lost time, the number of points built per iteration will probably stay flat or climb slowly.

For tracking and management purposes, treat the number as a fact of nature. If you're getting nine points per iteration, plan for nine.

So what about your release? Just do the math. Want to know what will be done six weeks from now, when you're doing nine points per two-week iteration? There are three iterations for 27 points. Pick the most valuable cards adding up to 27 points—that's your best estimate of what will be done.

Note why we say always to put the most valuable stories into each iteration. By choosing the most valuable stories, we make sure that the system has the highest value on any given day, including that most important day, release day!

Isn't it possible to be more accurate? Wouldn't it be better to build a PERT chart, or to use your favorite project manager to build a dependency graph? Well, in a word, no.[1] You're dealing with inherently unreliable data, namely the difficulty of software which is not yet written. You can't get decimal-place accuracy from your estimates, and there's no use trying. Estimate difficulty, measure performance, refine the estimates. That's the way to know what's going to happen.

And there's something more important than knowing what's going to happen—guiding what actually happens. It's not possible to control how long a given story takes, although we give some tips on doing your best in *Steering the Iteration* on page 151. What you can do—what you must do in our opinion—is control scope. By deciding what to do next and what to defer, you can have a system that does what it must do, with the best features possible, within the time and resources you have. There is no better deal than that.

Summary

Steering the release is the most critical aspect of XP. No matter how fast or slow the team is and no matter what happens as you go along, your best shot at a successful release by your scheduled date is to steer. Fortunately, steering is easy. Know what's done, know how fast your team is moving, and use that knowledge to decide what to do next and what to defer.

---

1. PERT and project software may do more harm than good. They give you the illusion of truth when all you have is estimates. They give you the illusion of control when all you have is data. They focus your attention on your computer screen instead of on your people. For an XP-sized project: *Resources, Scope, Quality, Time* (page 135). That's all you need. Do we repeat ourselves? Then we repeat ourselves.

Chapter 22

Handling Defects

Report 'em, schedule 'em, test and fix 'em, avoid 'em. Just don't call 'em bugs.

Call them Incident Reports or Customer Information Requests if you like. Just don't call them bugs. Bugs are things that creep into your software against your will. Every defect in your code was put there by one of the programmers. Two of the programmers, with pair programming. With the customers we visit, when something goes wrong, they think it's a defect. We'll talk here about reporting the problem, scheduling the repair, testing and fixing the problem, and avoiding as many defects as possible. But first, a word from our sponsor.

Defects reduce the value of the software to the customer. That runs counter to our primary purpose, which is delivering value to the customer. Defects also get in the way of delivering future value, by taking time that could have been used to do new things. Finally, defects that get through to the customer slow us down disproportionately. Since we don't have a test that shows the defect, it is often harder and more time-consuming to fix.

OK. We don't want defects. Hold that thought while we deal with them.

Reporting Problems

The users are on line and perhaps in their own space, away from you. They may want an easy way to submit problem reports. If they want to use e-mail, that's OK. If they ask you to build a problem reporting tool right into the software, that's OK too. The question is what do you do with those e-mails when you get them.

Write them on cards. That's right. You already have a good scheduling mechanism. Why not use it?[1] Let's go on to...

Scheduling Corrections

If the problem is of low enough priority, the customer can just write it on a card (or someone can), and schedule the fix in a future iteration. This is by far the best thing to do, as it uses your normal practiced flow of planning. Where possible, write the problems on cards and schedule them like any other story.

More urgent problems are a bit more complex. They need to be addressed in the current iteration, typically right away. Often that means that some already scheduled work won't get completed. What

---

1. Some folks want to have a defect database. We call that a defeatist attitude. On a greenfield project you may well be able to do without. Give it a try!

should be deferred? That, of course, is up to the customer. You'll need to communicate proactively on this because you won't even know how long it will take to fix the problem until you're nearly done. If you're dealing with a flow of defects, be sure you know your story and task priorities, and be sure you keep the customer up-to-date on the impact of your bug hunting. Consider putting a maximum amount of time on hunting before you consult the customer. They might want to reduce the priority of the defect if it's going to take a long time.

Keep track of the time spent fixing defects. Graph it on the wall. It's a potentially important consumption of resources and well worth watching. When you get some history on your velocity in the presence of defect fixes, use that velocity figure in planning the next iteration. As always, past history is your best indicator of future performance. But keep the defect time broken out and displayed. It may be taking a big bite of your development time, and if it is, you want to know it and do something about it.

When the flow of support issues is high enough, some XP teams dedicate programmers to support and fixes, usually on some kind of rolling schedule. Feel free to try this, as it has the advantage of letting the bulk of the programmers focus on new value without interruptions. There is an important downside to this approach, however: it reduces feedback in your process. By masking the impact of problems, you lose quite a bit of the incentive to avoid them. Some teams like to have defects sting a bit as they come in, to help remind them not to send them out.

Test and Fix the Problem

When a defect gets out to the customer, it slipped through both nets of tests, the unit tests and the acceptance tests. The best way to properly fix a defect is to start with a test that doesn't work and then fix it. So write a test to show the bug. Er, *defect*.

Customers, your acceptance tests let the defect through as well. While the problem is fresh in your memory, specify new tests for that problem and anything it brings to mind. This is your chance to avoid some irritation in the future. Programmers, do the same with the unit tests. There's a really good chance that when you do this, you'll both find additional problems. That's great—those are problems that won't come back to slow you down later. Don't let the press of time urge you to skip the tests. It will just slow you down later. Testing makes the whole project go faster and lets it deliver more value.

Preventing Defects

Let's face it, the fewer problems we have, the better we're going to like it. It's not realistic to expect no problems, but it's not healthy to get complacent. Sure, there are defects in almost all software. So, let's not get too excited when there are defects in ours. Maybe we're afraid that if defects aren't inevitable, defects in our code will mean we aren't as good as we should be. Well, we've all worked hard to get where we are, so we probably are as good as we should be. But unless we've stopped learning, we aren't as good as we could be. We aren't as good as we can be.

As an individual and as a team, look regularly at the defects that have turned up. Look at them from two angles: where did they come from and how could you prevent problems like them in the future.

Where did they come from? One thing is almost certain: a bunch of them will show up right at the edges of your testing. Problems will show up right at the edge of your input testing and downstream of your last output check. Some of these, even if they're many, will look as if there's nothing you can do.

"If they send us bad data, there's nothing we can do about it." We wish we were collecting a royalty on that sentence. It's used all over the world, and we'd be rich today. Often, however, there is something you can do. Tighten up your validity tests, do some early cross-checking or hash totals. Let your mind run a bit. Tightening this up will make your life easier.

There's another common event when you look at where the problems are coming from. Often there's a part of the system where they seem to cluster. This is your clue to do a little scrambling in that area. Maybe you need more tests there. Maybe a little refactoring is in order. Figure out what's needed, and give the area a little attention.

One more thing—often a team will notice a defect cluster in an area where there hasn't been pair programming. Yes, it's true. Many teams stop pairing occasionally, often in highly specialized areas. Take a look at your defect sources. If they show more problems where there has been less pairing—well, think about it. Maybe even do something about it.

Summary

That's the scoop on defects. Report them, schedule them, test to fix them, and prevent them. Go now, and bug no more!

Advanced Issue: Defect Databases

After release, if you have multiple users reporting problems, you clearly need some mechanism to keep track of them. If you have lots of users, writing on a card may not do. In December 1999, Ron was involved in a newsgroup conversation. Here, he is addressing whether a defect database is needed during active, prerelease, full XP development.

Ken asked:

> *Defect tracking will allow you to uncover "smells" in code (to use a refactoring phrase). If there are a large number of problems in a particular segment of your project, then you may want to focus on that segment and stabilize it. How do you identify this clustering unless you keep track of the errors. For example: we have 50 percent of our errors relating to monthly payroll.*

Yes, the potential problem is real. If there are a large number of problems in some area (even over time), then that area will need focus. Ken asks a good question: how do you keep track of this clustering?

Suppose some class, *BadClass*, hasn't been well tested and is poorly written. It's a defect cluster. It can and does happen.

How are the defects that cluster in *BadClass* detected and found? Or, rephrasing the question slightly, and I hope harmlessly, how do the existing XP practices naturally identify and deal with defect clusters?

Susie and Bill, using *BadClass* as they build more function, encounter those defects, which show up when their unit tests stop working because of a problem in *BadClass*.

XP has collective code ownership. So Susie and Bill fix *BadClass*. To do this, they need to have a unit test for BadClass that is failing.

All its tests work now, so they write one that shows the defect. They fix the defect.

Similarly, an acceptance test may show the problem. Someone has that story and needs to make it run. They find that *BadClass* is failing. Again, they write a unit test and fix *BadClass*.

Fixing *BadClass*, Susie and Bill notice that the code is ugly. They may refactor it a little, or they might make a note to do it later.

At the next stand-up meeting (no more than 24 hours away), they report what they're doing. Because they're a little ticked off about *BadClass* biting them, they mention it. Everyone gets a little nudge that *BadClass* is in fact bad.

BadClass is a defect cluster, so others have been bitten by *Bad-Class*, and they join in the grousing.

Soon, a couple of people will say, "*BadClass* has been ticking us off long enough. Let's go after it," and they'll do just that.

So the normal effect of relentless testing and collective code ownership and daily stand-up meeting is that the defects in *Bad-Class* get found early and often, and the whole team gets an awareness of where the problems are.

That's how the XP practices naturally identify and deal with defect clusters.

During the active implementation of the system, then, the whole team *tends* to know what's bad, and the bad *tends* to heal.

Might this be enough to ensure that there will in fact be no defect clusters? Well, it could happen. In my experience, it *does* happen. The team knows where the system is weak and they go after the weak places as a natural part of their work.

Because the existing XP rules and practices "automatically" attack and eliminate defect clusters, I question whether a defect database would carry its weight.

But Ken goes on:

Process improvement is about feeding the loop. XP starts this by including unit tests when bugs are discovered.

Yes. And the XP value of Simplicity suggests that a team might well start with the core practices and improve their practices where they need it, rather than assume they will need it and add weight to the process from the beginning. That's where I'm coming from. I'd strive to keep the defect count low enough to avoid the slower feedback from the database. But when I needed the database, I'd get one.

There are other elements that could be picked up from the other camps.

Unquestionably. The trick in XP, because you want to go fast, is to add only process elements that are actually needed and that will deliver more benefit than they cost.

During development, before there are multiple streams of support requests, I sincerely question whether a database would be needed. I know of lots of successful XP projects that don't have them.

If it were me, starting a greenfield project that would be delivered to many customers, I'd still start without a defect database because I don't think it'd be helpful during development.

I would be planning to buy or build something by the time the program got released to its targeted customer base.

YMMV, and if you use a database, you won't lose your XP merit badge. But remember the Courage value, try the practices clean, and watch for where you need process improvement. The real world will surely surprise both of us.

Advanced Practice: Tests as Database

Here's a tip from Chet on keeping track of defects by using process elements you already have: your tests. Stop relying on a trail of paper or e-mails, or even a database, to keep track of defects. Instead, write tests to show defects. You will need to decide how you will implement a test-driven defect list. Since the unit tests must be kept at 100 percent, you must decide how to have tests that document current bugs. There are four ways to do this:

1. Define defect tests as acceptance tests (which may be below 100 percent).
2. Keep the defect tests in a separate unit test category and shift them into the production unit suite as they are worked on.
3. Defer writing the test until you are ready to begin working on the defect. This can mean that the test will never get written, which isn't a good thing.
4. Or, the most fiendish way, take the failing test and release it into the production test suite and let it lay in wait for the next team of programmers to come along with code to release. They will discover the failure while running the production release suite and be forced to fix it before legally releasing their code. Moo ha ha ha.

When the team responsible for capturing defects finds one, they do enough analysis to be able to reproduce it in a test. The test is then passed along to the team responsible for fixing the defect. The correction team now has a concrete example of the failure and are able to work in the standard "write the test first" mode.

You're doing this right when defects are corrected quickly, without excessive meetings and confusion about what the defect report meant.

Chapter 23

Conclusion

We have been working with Extreme Programming for over four years and would never go back to what we did before. XP has equipped us to communicate better with our peers, our customers, and our managers. It has helped us to manage the stresses of working hard on something we deeply care about. We think it's good stuff, and we recommend it to anyone working on a project of suitable size and scope.

The values of XP are simplicity, communication, feedback, and courage. There's certainly enough to XP to fill this book and several others, yet the essence truly is simple. Be together with your customer and your fellow programmers, and talk with each other. Use simple design and programming practices, and simple methods of planning, tracking, and reporting. Test your program and your practices, using feedback to decide how to steer the project. Working together in this way gives the team courage. We've found that many of the higher-ceremony trappings of software projects are based on fear of the unknown—that fear is reduced or eliminated by XP's high communication, reducing the need for those practices. We've found that many such practices are based on fear of losing—we prefer to focus on winning, by delivering what the customer wants, when he wants it, in a context of solid software engineering.

There are 12 key practices in Extreme Programming, and we have addressed them all in as much detail as our ability and space have permitted. The practices are

- ❖ *On-Site Customer* (page 17);
- ❖ *Small Releases* (page 49);
- ❖ Planning, addressed in *Story Estimation* (page 37), *Customer Defines Release* (page 55), and *Iteration Planning* (page 61), and in the steering chapters: *Steering* (page 147), *Steering the Release* (page 157), and *Steering the Iteration* (page 151);
- ❖ Metaphor, addressed briefly in *Programming*, in the discussion of names on page 71;
- ❖ Simple design, addressed in *Quick Design Session* (page 69) and *Code Quality* (page 83), as well as in *Simple Design* (page 75) in the *Programming* chapter;
- ❖ *Pair Programming* (page 87);
- ❖ *Collective Code Ownership* (page 75);

- ❖ *Continuous Integration* (page 78);
- ❖ *Coding Standard* (page 79);
- ❖ Testing, addressed in *Acceptance Tests* (page 31), *Unit Tests* (page 93), and other chapters;
- ❖ *Refactoring* (page 76), for which you really need Martin Fowler's book, *Refactoring*;
- ❖ *Forty-Hour Week* (page 81).

The rules and practices we have described here are not intended to be followed blindly, although we do sincerely recommend that you start by following the practices closely. What's really important, though, is not to work as if XP is a checklist but, instead, let it get into your bones. Just as an XP project controls itself by steering—making small adjustments as you go—the application of XP in your environment should be the same. Get the feeling for what is happening in your organization, get the data, then adjust your process, keeping in mind simplicity, communication, feedback—and courage.

To become truly good at programming is a life's work, an ongoing enterprise of learning and practicing. To become good at Extreme Programming is much the same. In spite of the name, Extreme Programming is about people as much as it is about programming, and our relationships with other people are what life itself should be about.

We have enjoyed the journey so far and sincerely hope that you will as well. If we can help—like the truth, we're out there. Look us up.

Bonus Tracks

Here are some things we've paid a lot to learn. Since you bought the album, we wanted to give you a little something extra. Thank you, and we hope we passed the audition.

Chapter 24

We'll Try

"We'll try" can be the saddest words a programmer has ever spoken, and most of us have spoken them more than once. We've covered this material in other forms already, but it bears repeating here.

"We'll try."

These words are often the preface to months of grueling effort against a deadline we know in our heart we cannot make. At the end, we come up tired, burnt out, beaten, and short. Management hates us, we hate ourselves, our families don't know us anymore or have fallen by the wayside. The software, if it works at all, is nothing to be proud of.

Oh, there have been exceptions. Successful products have been launched this way, and there is a certain pride in having gone through hell and survived. We have to believe it was worth it, if the alternative is to believe we wasted a big chunk of our lives.

There has to be a better way. Here's one that couldn't really happen.

Suppose you knew everything they were asking for, and suppose you knew how long it would take your team to do every one of the things they were asking for.

Suppose you knew that, and you weren't afraid of the truth. Suppose you wrote down everything they were asking for, maybe on little cards, and you went in to them and laid your cards on the table.

Suppose you said: Here's everything you have asked for, and on each card I've put down how long it is going to take to get done. I've broken them down into three-week periods, and in each period I've put as many cards as will get done in that period. As you can see, it will take 14 periods to do all this.

You lay a pencil vertically between two of the columns, and say: "Here's the date we want to deliver. We have too much to do. Our job now is to put the cards we want the most on the left side of the pencil. When we put a card over there, we have to remove a card with the same number on it."

They rant. They rave. They call you names. Secure in your perfect knowledge, you say, This is how long each of these things will take. To get the best product by our date, we need to put the cards we want most on the left side of the pencil, removing cards with the same number.

They threaten your job. You say, trying not to smile, "This is how long it will take our current team to do it. Maybe if you fire us, you can find, recruit, hire, and train a team that will get it done sooner."

Bask for a moment in how calm, strong, totally cool, and heroic you would be, because you know how long it will take.

But that couldn't happen, could it? Yes, it could. We may not be able to do as well as the lucky devil above, but it turns out we can do pretty well. Here's how an XP team does it:

For a moment, get in touch with that feeling you have when you're just coding along. The world goes away, you code and test and test and code, and quickly you're done with whatever it is.

A day of that is what we call a perfect engineering day. For a lot of your tasks, you probably have a solid feeling: If you guys would just leave me alone, I could do that in two days!

Cool. With that in hand, we only need three things:

1. We need to know all the things we have to do.
2. We need to have that solid feeling for each of them.
3. We need to know how many real days it takes to get a perfect engineering day.

Armed with that information, a stack of cards, and a pencil, we can estimate how long any project will take!

It Couldn't Be That Easy!

It isn't exactly easy, but it isn't hard. Briefly, here's how an XP team goes about it.

First, we have to have the user stories on cards. It would be nice to have all of them. It's important to have enough of them, and to write placeholder cards for stories that don't exist yet.

The entire team, customers and programmers, goes through all the stories. Customers explain what the system has to do, and the team brainstorms quickly how it might be done. Estimate each card in programmer weeks: one, two, or three weeks of one programmer's time.

If a story seems much less than a week, batch it with a few other small ones. If it seems more than three weeks, take that as a sign that you don't understand it. Get the customers to break it down into two or more stories and explain it again. Repeat until you have all the stories estimated.

Now no one believes we can do all those stories in the time we estimate, because there is so much else to do that we haven't counted. We'll start by assuming we are off by a factor of three. Yes, three! We'll guess that it takes us three weeks to do what we could do in one perfect week. If that's too conservative, we'll know soon enough and reflect it in future plans. We call our actual speed of delivering stories *velocity*, and this figure is a velocity adjustment to use until we know our real velocity. We're assuming a velocity of one-third story point per programmer per week.

Pick an iteration size (we'll use three weeks) and figure out how many programmer weeks there are in an iteration: three weeks 3 *N* programmers divided by three. (We divided our factor of three back out. If we had guessed 2, we'd have divided by 2.)

Voila, you plan for one week's work done in every iteration, for each of your *N* programmers! This is a really good starting point.

Start arranging cards into groups of *N* (the number of programmers) points' work. Each of these piles will take, we estimate, three weeks to get done. Count the piles, check the calendar. That's your prediction for when you'll get done.

Of course, no one believes this. But we're doing to do it again and again, as we go along in the project. And we're going to refine our ability to estimate, and we're going to learn more about how the system works, so we will know more about how long things will take. A little way into the project, we'll be really good at this. Better yet, because we will be tracking this performance, management will come to know that we are really good at it, and they'll start believing our estimates.

At this point you might be asking yourself some questions.

What if You Don't Have All the Stories?

Don't worry—you can be sure you don't have all the stories. It's important to at least have placeholders for all the big ones. Spend a little time brainstorming, customers and programmers together, about what else might be needed. Make cards for the things that make sense. Estimate them like all the others. But the specific stories aren't as important as the steering that becomes possible when you can tell the customer how fast you are going.

How Do You Get Estimates? [1]

Estimating is scary. Assume for now that no one will know but you what you come up with. We'll talk about how to deal with errors shortly.

With all the programmers together, estimates will tend to average out. And remember: we have our velocity adjustment to give us some slack, and we will be revising the schedule many times as we go along.

---

1. In this book, there's more about estimation in *Iteration Planning* (page 61), *Experience Improves Estimates* (page 131), and *How to Estimate Anything* (page 185).

Programmers divide up into teams of two or three. Each team looks at each story. Reflect on how you are going to do it in the system, using your experience in general, and any exploration already done, to guide you. Talk through an option, and estimate how long each step would take.

Consider alternatives. If you think of an easier alternative, or someone says they think they can do it in less time, take the smaller number. When the other teams look at a card that has already been estimated, they can reduce the time but not increase it.

If you can't estimate a story because there's something you don't know, something not yet figured out, put down the one you can't estimate, pick up the precursor, and estimate it. Get back to the dependent story.

Repeat until all teams have looked at all stories. If you take ten minutes per story, you can do 150 stories in three days. You'll probably wind up going faster than that after the first few.

How Do You Explain Velocity?

We recommend that you start with a velocity of one-third story point per programmer per week. That is, we assume that every week of time you estimate for development will take three weeks of real time.

This number is a rule of thumb. An experienced XP team will have a measured, more accurate number, and you'll be experienced real soon.

Here are some of the things that make up the number. There are probably more.

You probably don't have all the stories, and some of the ones you do have will change as customers learn more about what they really need.

There will be meetings, reports, writing, support, testing, planning, and various other activities that mean no one will really be able to program eight hours a day, day in and day out.

You don't know your real velocity yet, and one-third is a fairly decent starting point.

We Can't Tell Management Our Real Estimates!

Some teams are afraid to tell management their "perfect engineering" estimates for the stories, for fear they will be held to those estimates instead of the loaded ones.

If this is your situation, use perfect engineering in your head, but call the estimates eXtreme Programming Units (XPUs) or something. One project called the estimates Gummi Bears, but it is probably better for the programmers to think in terms of their own perfect time.

Then it is simple enough to say to management: "In each three-week period, each programmer can do one XPU. eXtreme Programming Units are carefully calibrated estimates of difficulty. We'll be measuring our rate of delivering XPUs as we go along, so you'll be able to track how we're doing."

This Can't Possibly Work!

You're asking how this could possibly work. The amazing thing is that it actually works pretty well, even for your first estimate of the project. But what makes it really work is that you do it again and again.

When you present your first release plan, explain to the management people how you got the schedule. Then tell them that you do not believe this schedule, and that neither should they. You go on:

"Many things can and will change in the course of this development. Customers will change requirements, some things will turn out to be easier than we thought, and some will be harder. That has happened in every project we have ever done, and it will happen this time.

"The difference with this project is that we will do this schedule every nine weeks as we go along, and we will report the results to you. We will refine all our estimates of the remaining stories, based on what we have learned in the preceding iterations. Each time we get together, we will all see how many stories are done, and how many there are to go.

"Each time we get together, expect to see that we are closer to completion. Expect also that the date may move in, and it may move out. But you will be able to see exactly what our estimate is, and that will enable you to make good decisions about the project.

"We're confident that we can give you quality information about how we're doing, and we're confident that with that information you will have the best chance of helping us be successful."

And you will do just that: you will observe your own performance, and you will estimate the stories over again based on what you know, and every two months your ability to estimate the schedule will get better and better.

Even better, customers and management will learn that you are telling the truth as you know it. They will learn that your estimate of the schedule is the best they can get; they will learn that they can help with the delivery by providing you what you need and by adjusting scope judiciously to help you make the date.

Not with My Management!

Sometimes teams believe that even with the best knowledge of what the schedule will really be, their management is so draconian, so unenlightened, so evil, that the process can't possibly work.

Well, if it's really that bad, I'd advise you to hit the silk.[2]

But more likely, management has been lied to, misled, bamboozled, and spun so many times that they have come to believe that nothing works but pressure.

Give the process a chance. Most managers really are more than ready to use accurate information to make better decisions. Every time you do this process, your knowledge of what will happen improves. If every time you report, you tell them what you really believe will happen, even the most dull management will finally figure out that your estimates are better than whatever they are shouting.

In January you'll say: "Here is our schedule, it shows we'll be done in September." They'll shout at you that it must be done in June. You say, "We'll try, but if this is what we have to do, it'll be September. That's with all three hundred points in there. Two hundred points we could do by June, if you'd like to reduce scope."

In March, you'll say: "Notice that we got done about what we predicted. Our schedule shows that we'll be done in September, or June on reduced scope." They'll shout, but they won't be so sure. Expect them to say you have to work harder. "We're working as effectively as we can," you reply. "Would you like to see our tracking report?"

Every month, your schedule shows you converging on the predicted date. It must: there's less to do each time, and your experience in estimating will inevitably improve. Even the most pointy-haired management will get it. And if they don't, you're still the best estimating, most effective team in the company. How can this be bad?

---

2. This is a reference to bailing out of an airplane. Used back when Jeffries was a boy.

Chapter 25

How to
Estimate Anything

Sometimes estimating stories seems scary. Keep your heads, stick together, and break the story down into small parts. You'll be surprised what you can do.

Let's look now at a complex story and see how we might break it down into tasks that can be estimated.

Psychic Message Management

All messages displayed by the Psychic Operating System will appear in overlapping rectangles. Each rectangle is independently clickable and will come to the front of the screen before the user actually clicks it. Owing to the importance of prime numbers in getting good psychic contact, all the rectangles must have their length and width be prime numbers. If the window is too small to hold the message, there should be a Psychic Extension Bar on the right side of the window.

I didn't promise a reasonable story and, in fact, didn't want one. Part of what we'll see here is that even a story that seems impossibly weird will yield to task breakdown, especially if the team works together. Help me out here. What are some of the tasks we have to do to implement the story? Speak up. We haven't implemented the Psychic Operating System yet.

1. Well, we have to be able to display rectangles on the screen. Regular windows are rectangular—wonder if that would work.
2. We have to put text inside the rectangles. There's a *TextBox* object or something like that, I think.
3. Sounds like the windows have a bar on the right side to scroll the message up and down. We could use a scroll bar for that.
4. The rectangles have to have prime length and width. We'll need a list of primes. I bet I can do that in a couple of hours.
5. The window has to come to the front before the user clicks on it. That could be tricky. Would it be OK if it came up just a little bit before he clicked on it? I've got an idea—what if the window popped up as soon as your mouse got near it?

These tasks are starting to look reasonable. They all seem to be possible, except for maybe number five, and it's not hard to estimate how to do them. For this story, some of them take minutes, so maybe we went too far. In most stories, it's enough to get the tasks down to a day or so.

Some very important things have happened here.

The team has translated the customer's requirement into something they can understand. At first, the idea seemed strange and impossible, but it turns out we actually understand it.

The team has taken a story they couldn't possibly estimate, and broken it down into finite tasks that they can actually estimate and do. This is design. An XP team does design throughout the project, and we just did a little bit of it here.

The tasks are mostly estimatable. The one that may not be easy to estimate is broken out as well, and someone already has an idea. We'll do an experiment.

A seemingly impossible story has turned into something we can predict and actually do. Not bad.

Chapter 26

Infrastructure

What about that database you need to build first? What about that framework? What about that syntax-directed command compiler? Get over it!

All too often, projects go dark for a few months at the beginning while the programmers build some absolutely necessary bit of infrastructure. Usually the team really believes that it's necessary, and that it will make things go faster in the long run.

YAGNI: "You Aren't Gonna Need It." This slogan, one of XP's most famous and controversial, reminds us always to work on the story we have, not something we think we're going to need. Even if we know we're going to need it.

XP's planning process works by allowing the customers to steer all the development, based on business value. If we wait for a few months while we are not delivering business value, we're violating that process and losing the customers' interest and confidence. We may never get it back. Some projects never emerge from this cave of darkness. Don't go in there.

Some teams address infrastructure by allowing some percentage of programmers' time to go to infrastructure tasks. "We need a database, so we'll put two programmers' worth of work on it in every iteration. That's two for us, and the remaining six for the customer." This is a bit better, but frankly, it's a slippery slope.

One project we know of took 100 percent of one of its final iterations on infrastructure issues. This really confused the customers, who had had stories in mind for that iteration. Doctor, it hurts when I confuse my customers.[1]

Where possible, associate infrastructure work with specific stories that the customer wants. One of our favorite examples is this one: the programmers realized that they needed to write some scripts to check whether input data files were available and FTP them to the server. They couldn't think of a way to associate this with business value.

Finally, someone got the answer. The story was "When we (the customers) show up in the morning at 8 A.M., the data is there live on our systems." Naturally, the customers wanted this—they gave it a very high priority. And this story served quite well as the basis for the tasks of writing the scripts.

Use this trick ruthlessly. Every time you are thinking of some big infrastructure investment that you may have to make "behind the scenes," tie it back to customer business value. If you can't, maybe the customer doesn't need it. If the customer doesn't need it, don't do it.

---

1. If you don't know this joke, e-mail us. No, on second thought, "Don't do that."

OK, you've got it tied to a story: "The system records name, address, age, height, weight, and a lot of other personal information for each of ten million patients. It can display any patient by record number and can display statistical analyses for any and all stored data. It knows everything that has ever happened to any patient at any time. And that's just the beginning."

Oops, clearly we need a database. Or do we?

First of all, that story is too big to estimate. Let's break it down. Here are a couple of the new stories:

"The system records name, address, age, height, and weight for patients."

"The system can display any patient."

"The system supports ten million patients."

OK, but doesn't that still imply a database? Well, yes, but maybe not right away. What if you wrote the initial system to know just those fields for a few patients and stored them on a file? Might you be able to deliver some value with such a system? Sure you could. Up to 1,000 patients, or even 10,000, it might work just fine on the file.

On a file, you could easily add fields or change their size or content: just write little programs to do it.

"Yes, but what about integrity?" you ask.

"Do you have a story for that?" we ask. "And how hard is integrity anyway?"

Files actually have very high integrity, especially if you're a little careful about writing them in the right order. You could go a long way on files.

But, honestly, we do know that sooner or later you're going to want to have a database. But if you are able to deliver business value for a few iterations without one, just writing the information to files and reading it back, the cool thing is that the database schema will stop changing so much. The record definitions, the fields, and the formats will stabilize as the customers get to see the system in operation. Once things stabilize, it's no big deal to go in and set up the database. Sure, it'll still happen that you need to change it, but you'll have most of the structure in hand, and refactorings won't be so frequent or severe.

But wait, won't it be really hard to convert the system to use the database after making it run on files? That could take ages!

Go back and read *Code Quality* on page 83, especially rule three, "Say everything once and only once." Quality, well-factored code for your file-based application will have just one place that reads each record type, and one place that writes it. Those places will converge down to just one place that reads an arbitrary record and just one that writes. Those are the places—the only places—where the database access code will have to go.

Now as you begin with XP, we realize you'll have trouble fully signing up for this philosophy. At first you'll feel the need to do some amount of infrastructure work, and you'll have to find some technique to avoid going completely dark on your client. Maybe the level of effort thing.

But where possible, associate infrastructure explicitly with customer value. And where possible, do infrastructure tasks very incrementally, a little bit with each story. When your courage is high, try extra simple solutions, then watch how they work out. If your anxiety level gets high, go ahead and put in as much generality as you think you need—but just enough for right now.

Observe what happens. We're sure you'll find that you don't need to invest as much in the future as you used to, and that things will actually go more smoothly in the process. As you go along, put more and more simplicity in at the beginning, relying on your ability to refactor to add the generality—or the general tools—that you'll need.

Chapter 27

It's Chet's Fault

Are you looking for someone to blame? This chapter explains how to know whose fault it is. Now move on and solve your problems.

Early on in the C3 project, the team was having a "discussion" about something that had gone wrong. Someone was trying to find out who had messed up. Chet got fed up with the witch-hunt and announced, "It's my fault." He took a card (we had a few around) and wrote "It's my fault" on it and signed it. Then he put it in his desk and told everyone where to find it if we ever needed someone to blame.

Everyone knew that it wasn't Chet's fault, which was what made his act so powerful. It jolted us all out of looking for *who* and back into looking for *what to do*. It reminded us that we were a team, on a team effort, and that we all accept responsibility for everything that happens. It was one of Chet's famous stone-snatching moves.[1]

Since then, other teams have taken advantage of it being Chet's fault. Some just use the same old Chet who is writing this book, but others have adopted their own Chet. Here's a picture of the real Chet and the Chet from a very special team in Omaha. See if you can guess who is who.

---

1. Another was the famous *Balancing Hopes and Fears* (page 195), where Chet snatched the stone from the very hand of Beck himself.

Chapter 28

Balancing
Hopes and Fears

*Those of you who have heard Ron, Ann, or me speak about XP
are probably wondering where all the war stories are. Well, here's
one.*

C3 was about ready to launch, the acceptance tests where in the low nineties and moving steadily upwards, performance was within acceptable levels. But we had one hole. Early in the project, we had decided to retain the reporting portions of the legacy system. This would allow us to control the new system's interface, and maybe to launch the first phase of the system much more quickly. Unfortunately, that interface contained several hundred poorly understood data items. And it is difficult to write acceptance tests when the customer doesn't know what the data means let alone what the correct values are.

So here we were, all of our measures were pointing to a launch in the near future, but we all knew that our biggest risk was not showing up on our charts. We knew it, but we didn't want to know it. And so we lied to ourselves, or at least we didn't tell ourselves the complete truth.

About this time Kent made one of his periodic visits and after assessing the situation, called us all together. We then had the most uncomfortable meeting I have ever attended. We had worked very hard, we had a program that did an obviously better job of calculating the payroll than the legacy system did, so we wanted to launch it. But we had to come to grips with the problems with the tapeworm (as the interface to the legacy reporting system was called). After about an hour of talking about our certainty that the calculations were correct, and our uncertainty as to whether we could communicate the results of those calculations to the program that would actually print the payroll checks, we adjourned. A couple of us stood around talking to Kent about what we should do next. I walked the couple of feet to where the acceptance tests results were posted and reflected on the meeting. I had an epiphany. I went back to where Kent was and said that we were just "balancing hopes and fears." We had focused on our hope that we could launch the system as planned and our fear that we wouldn't. Kent told me that I had just "snatched the pebble from the master's hand."

We knew what had to be done. Kent called everyone back. We brainstormed the tasks that were required to launch the system, estimated them, and started back to work with a schedule we all believed in. We still had some uncertainty about the tapeworm, but we had given ourselves permission to talk about it.

We had let our emotions rule our actions, so much so that we had co-opted Kent into our emotional state. Because we had allowed this major piece of functionality to be developed outside the mainstream of our process, it had no acceptance tests. We had no way of knowing how close it was to being finished and no way of measuring its progress toward completion except for days expended. This lack of knowledge caused us to become afraid of the tapeworm, and as we know, "Fear leads to Anger. Anger leads to Hate. Hate leads to Suffering."

Chapter 29

Testing Improves Code

An example showing how writing some tests can help you to improve the code.

My favorite coding partner, Rich Garzaniti, and I were writing an object to control the printing of checks and EFT stubs from the C3 payroll system. We had a collection of *Disclosure* objects, each of which knew all the information required to print each document. Our next task was to split the creation of the actual print files into multiple concurrent processes. The disclosures were in the correct order for printing and check numbers had been assigned, so all we had to do was write a little code to split the collection into equal chunks and parcel it out to each process. We wrote a method on the object responsible for controlling multithreaded processes.

```
SharedManagedPopulation>>intervalToProcess
    | slice start end |
    slice := disclosures size // numberOfThreads.
    start := (slice * threadNumber - 1) + 1.
    end := (start + slice) max: disclosures size.
    ^Interval
        from: start
        to: end
```

We had written a little workspace code to make sure we had the algorithm right, but now we needed to write a unit test. The method we had written was self-contained; all the information we had needed was stored as instance variables on the class. To test it we would have to create a series of *SharedManagedPopulations,* each with a collection of *Disclosures,* each with the appropriate *numberOfThreads* and *threadNumber.* That seemed like too much work to us, so we decided to refactor the code to make it easier to test.

```
SharedManagedPopulation>>intervalForThread: threadInteger
    numberOfThreads: threadTotalInteger
    collectionSize: sizeInteger

    |slice start end|
    slice := sizeInteger // threadTotalInteger.
    Start := (slice * threadInteger) + 1.
    End := (start + slice) max: sizeInteger.
    ^Interval
        from: start
        to: end
```

```
SharedManagedPopulation>>intervalToProcess
    ^self
        intervalForThread: threadNumber
        numberOfThreads: numberOfThreads
        collectionSize: disclosures size
```

The need to test the *intervalToProcess* method easily had caused us to remove its interesting behavior to the new helper method *interval-ForThread:numberOfThreads:collectionSize:*. The result was that *interval-ToProcess* no longer needed a test, since it had no behavior and therefore could not fail. *intervalForThread:numberOfThreads:collectionSize:* could be tested without any setup beyond creating an instance of *Shared-ManagedPopulation*.

The pressure to test forced us to write better code. This is a pattern we have encountered time and again during our XP experience: code that cannot be easily tested is not factored properly. This happens because we are breaking an XP rule: Write the tests first. If we had written the unit test first, instead of using an experiment written in a workspace, we would have discovered the need for the helper method much sooner.

Does this mean Rich and I are bad people? No, it just means we are people. And it also means this lesson has two morals. If you are having difficulty writing the test, refactor the code to split out the behavior. Second, if you find yourself needing to split out the behavior to improve testability, write the test first. In either case, you will discover that testing will improve the quality of your code.

Chapter 30

XPer Tries Java

After the C3 project ended, most of the team was transferred to work on the human resources intranet. I found how they were using the principles of XP to improve their lives on a new project heartening. What follows is a description of how Rich Garzaniti, exC3er and devoted XPer, is introducing testing and modern development tools into an environment where none existed.

One of the first tasks on my new assignment was to change an intranet Web application to access a different directory service. The application had been born four years earlier and was using its own Lightweight Directory Access Protocol (LDAP) directory server to access corporate data. In the intervening four years, the corporation had developed a central corporate LDAP directory server which was far more accurate.

A change to use one LDAP over another sounds easy, right? Just change a parameter or two and off you go. What I found was anything but. The layouts of the two directory servers were different.

The application was written in Server-Side Java Script (SSJS). It used live connect technology to communicate with Java objects on the server. These Java objects were responsible for interfacing with the directory server and returning information to the application. The application used Netscape's Directory SDK. Our Java class *LdapServer* created an instance of *LdapConnection*, passed it some parameters, and received back a *UserData* object that contained the result of the LDAP query.

The first attempt at making and testing this change was a nightmare. The connection parameters resided in one of the Java classes. A duplicate file directory structure was copied on the test Unix server to accommodate the changes being made to the SSJS and the Java classes. Changes to the files were being made using vi on the test machine. Since the test server did not have the correct environment to test the change (no comment on this one), the files were then moved to a preproduction machine. A make-file was run that compiled and linked all the associated files together. The Web server then had to be stopped and restarted for the changes to take effect. The Web browser then was engaged through a special port (set up for testing) that started the application.

This was totally unacceptable. Each code change required five to ten minutes to verify its effects. Three developers spent three days mucking around in all this code. The only error message displayed in the browser was 'Exception 52' (translated: The LDAP server is unavailable). The end result was three days of frustration and nothing accomplished (except knowing what a 52 LDAP exception is). As a bonus, all that hacking and slashing of files and directories corrupted the already unstable environment, and the server was unavailable for over a week.

What we were missing were some good testing tools. The developers in the group were used to writing applications in scripting languages like SSJS and PERL. And boy did they love coding in vi! Coming from a Smalltalk environment, I was used to working in a great IDE and being able to step through *running* code to help debug problems. So I knew there had to be another way.

I purchased a copy of Visual Age for Java Professional Edition (VAJ) and installed it on my PC. I then went to the XProgramming site and downloaded the JUnit testing framework. I imported the framework into VAJ and spent a few hours familiarizing myself with it. I had spent three years using the Smalltalk version, so the mechanics of how it worked were pretty easy to follow.

Having used ENVY/Developer for many years, I was also familiar with the paradigm on which VAJ operated. I immediately felt the power of knowing that all the Java code I wrote would be in a code repository and I wouldn't be dealing with files all over the place. And version control would be greatly simplified.

Our application's interface to LDAP was localized through Java classes. The first thing I did was try to import the three classes that had been developed specifically for the application. The exceptions I got trying to import stated that *netscape.ldap.** was not visible. I then went to the Netscape Web site and downloaded the Directory SDK. It came with two *jar* files that contained all *the.class* files from the SDK. So, as a first step I imported the *jar* files into VAJ. No problems there. I then tried again to import our three application classes. Success! At least they were imported without any errors.

The next step was to browse the code and try to make a little sense of how it all operated so I could start writing some unit tests. The two immediate advantages I had at this point were being in a good editor and having VAJ browser tools at my disposal. Unlike the generic vi program, the ability to double-click inside a pair of {} brackets and have the entire block of code between them highlighted made reading code much easier. The availability of the search tools in VAJ was what really made things fly. Being able to open a class browser on referenced classes and find senders and implementers of methods in a unified environment makes you realize that there is no other way to do it.

I have to admit that within an hour I had a much better knowledge of how the code all fit together than I had after three days of looking at Java code in vi in different files and trying to piece it all together. (As you can tell, I am a tool guy.)

It was now time to write a unit test. I figured I should be able to get a simple test written that used the untouched imported code to connect to our own LDAP and return a *UserData* object. Since I was running VAJ on my local Windows 95 PC and the LDAP directories were on our pre-production unix servers, I first thought I would have to set up some kind of local LDAP test server. But I decided against that strategy. One of our XP mottoes was "let Smalltalk tell you." Even though this was Java, I knew that if there were a problem, the code would tell me. I knew how VAJ worked and that it would actually help me find any problems.

First, I built a test case called *LDAPTest* (subclassed from *TestCase*). I then took the SSJS code that instantiated an *LdapServer* object and put it in the *setUp()* method of the test:

```
public void setUp() {
    ldapServer = new LdapServer();
}
```

The constructor on *LdapServer* creates and opens a connection to the actual LDAP directory server.

I then wrote a simple test method:

```
public void testLdap() {
    UserData data = ldapServer.getUserData("t9999rg");
    assertEquals(data.emplId(), "666666");
}
```

Since I had configured VAJ with JUnit as a tool, I simply right-clicked on the *LdapTest* class and selected Tools >Junit. The JUnit GUI opens and automatically runs the test. The best part of all this was that the progress bar came up green; the test had run! And it ran in 0.054 seconds. A few hours of work and I now had a repeatable test that would test any changes I made to the LDAP classes. I think that is a good thing. I then expanded the number of assertions to test every piece of data the *UserData* object is supposed to retrieve.

Now that the test was up and running, I placed a breakpoint at the start of the test and was able to step through the running code. There is no better way to decipher how an application works than to watch it do its thing. The reaction from other members of the team was immediate. They realized that debugging time in this environment would be only one-tenth of what it was currently. After watching me for that one day writing tests and stepping through code, another member of the team took a small Java application he had written, imported the code into VAJ, and spent time walking step-by-step through the code he had written.

Now I set my sights on the task at hand. I needed to change the code to point to the new corporate LDAP directory server. The *Ldap-Server* creates an instance of *LdifServer* which actually does the LDAP interfacing. After reviewing how *LdifServer* worked (by stepping through the unit tests), I realized that a refactoring of the class was needed to proceed. With my unit tests in place, I knew it would be a snap.

Here is what *LdifServer* looked like before I started:

```java
private void openConnection() {
    _conn = new LDAPConnection();
    try {
        _conn.connect("oddshpr1-nf0.oddc.company.com", 389);
        _base = "o=American Corporation, c=US";
        _scope = LDAPv3.SCOPE_SUB;
    }
    catch(Exception ex) {
        System.out.println(ex);
        return;
    }
}

public UserData getUserData(String tid) {
    openConnection();
    String filter = "(&(objectclass=companyPerson)"
                    +"(uid=" +tid +"))";
    String attrs[] = { "givenName", "sn", "employeeNumber",
                    "nationality", "destinationIndicator",
                    "cn", "employeeType", "dsHasAgreed" };
    boolean attrsOnly = false;
    LDAPSearchConstraints cons = _conn.getSearchConstraints();
    LDAPSearchResults results;
    UserData data = null;
    try     {
        results = _conn.search(_base,_scope, filter, attrs,
                    attrsOnly, cons);

        if(!results.hasMoreElements()) return(null);

        LDAPEntry entry = results.next();
        LDAPAttributeSet attribs = entry.getAttributeSet();

        String  givenName = getValue(attribs, 0);
        String  sn = getValue(attribs, 1);
        String  employeeNumber = getValue(attribs, 2);
        String  nationality = getValue(attribs, 3);
```

```
            String  plant = getValue(attribs, 4);
            String  cn = getValue(attribs, 5);
            String  employeeType = getValue(attribs, 6);
            boolean isEmployee =
                !(employeeType.equalsIgnoreCase("N/A"));
            boolean policyFlag = getValue(attribs,
                                7).equalsIgnoreCase("true");
            data = new UserData(tid, givenName, sn, null,
                    isEmployee, employeeNumber, nationality, plant,
                    cn, employeeType, policyFlag);
        }
    catch(Exception ex) {
        try {
            System.out.println("Exception: " +ex );
        }
        catch(Exception ex2) {
        }
    }
    return(data);
}
```

As you can see, the code was a mess. Not only was it hard to follow, but the individual pieces were impossible to test. Without getting into too much detail on how the LDAP interface works, the *LdapConnection* executes a *search()* function that takes a whole bunch of parameters. These parameters specify which Ldap directory server to connect to and what attributes to retrieve. It was obvious that refactoring the search attributes would make it possible to subclass *LdifServer* and override the connection parameters.

Here's what I ended up with:

```
private void connect() {
    try {_conn.connect(ldapServer(), ldapPort());
    }
    catch(Exception ex) {systemOut(ex);
    }
}

public String ldapServer() {
    return "oddshpr1-nf0.oddc.company.com";
}

public int ldapPort() {
    return 389;
}
```

I then subclassed *LdifServer* into *CorporateLdifServer* and overrode one method:

```
public String ldapServer() {
    return "directory.appl.company.com";
}
```

Since I had written my new unit test, I just hit the Run button and, what do you know, the test ran! That wasn't so hard. I decided to refactor the other method so I could test it thoroughly.

```
public UserData getUserData(String tid) {
    LDAPSearchResults results = null;
    LDAPEntry entry = null;

    try {results = search(tid);}
    catch(Exception ex) {systemOut(ex);}

    if(!results.hasMoreElements()) return(null);

    try {entry = results.next();}
    catch(Exception ex) {systemOut(ex);}

    UserData data = newUserData(entry);
    return(data);
}
public LDAPSearchResults search(String tid) {
    LDAPSearchResults results = null;
    try {results = _conn.search(ldapBase(),
        ldapScope(),
        ldapFilter(tid),
        ldapAttributes(),
        ldapAttributesOnly(),
        ldapSearchConstraints());}
    catch(Exception ex) {systemOut(ex );}
    return(results);
}
```

I was now able to write more unit tests for each piece of the puzzle. Here are a few examples:

```
public void testLdapConnections() {
    LdifServer ldifServer = new LdifServer();
    assert(ldifServer.connection().isConnected());

    try {ldifServer.connection().disconnect();}
    catch(Exception ex){};
```

```
        assert(!ldifServer.connection().isConnected());

        try {ldifServer.connection().connect(ldifServer.l
dapServer(),
            ldifServer.ldapPort());}
        catch(Exception ex){};

        assert(ldifServer.connection().isConnected());
        assertEquals(ldifServer.ldapPort(), 389);
        assertEquals(ldifServer.ldapScope(), 2);
        assertNull(ldifServer.ldapAttributes());
        assert(!ldifServer.ldapAttributesOnly());
        assertNull(ldifServer.newUserData(null));
    }

    public void testLdapSearch() {
        LdifServer ldifServer = new LdifServer();
        LDAPSearchResults results = ldifServer.search("t4321rg");
        assert(results.hasMoreElements());
    }

    public void testNullLdapSearch() {
        LdifServer ldifServer = new LdifServer();
        UserData data = ldifServer.getUserData("TestNullReturn");
        assertNull(data);
    }
```

After more refactoring and more tests, we were ready to move from the test environment to real time. I exported the *.class* files from Visual Age and replaced the ones on the server. Then I logged into the application. To my complete and utter lack of surprise, it worked! This compared to three days of hassle on the previous attempt with NO success and no clues. A day's worth of coding, testing, and refactoring had gotten the job done.

In the course of making these changes, it was announced that there was to be a new and improved corporate directory server making its debut in three weeks. This time, the server we were using wasn't changing, but all the attribute names were! With all the refactoring work that I had done, I was able to make the change and test this new piece in 15 minutes. And I know when it comes time to turn it over, it will be a nonevent.

Chapter 31

A Java Perspective

We would like to thank Bill Wake for allowing us to use this article. It is the second in a series entitled "The Test/Code Cycle in XP." His website, http://users.vnet.net/wwake, contains the entire series plus a whole lot more.

People who unit-test, even many who unit-test in Extreme Programming, don't necessarily test the user interface. You can use JUnit to assist in this testing, however. This paper will work through a small but plausible example, giving the flavor of testing and programming using JUnit. This paper is part two, but can be read on its own; part one developed the model.

Example

Suppose we're developing a simple search engine. We'd like the user interface to look something like this:

We'll develop it in the XP style, working back and forth between testing and coding.

Model First

When you're creating a GUI, you should develop and test the model first. We'll assume this has been done and that it has the following interface:

```
public class SearcherFactory {
    public static Searcher get(String s)
            throws IOException {...}
}

public interface Searcher {
    public Result find(Query q);
}

public class Query {
    public Query(String s) {...}
    public String getValue() {...}
}
public interface Result {
    public int getCount();
    public Document getItem(int i);
}

public interface Document {
    public String getAuthor();
    public String getTitle();
    public String getYear();
}
```

In testing and developing the GUI, I don't mind depending on the *interfaces* of the model; I'm less happy when I have to depend on its concrete classes.

The GUI Connection

What we'd like to have happen:

❖ a searcher is associated with the GUI
❖ a query is entered

✧ the button is clicked

✧ the table fills up with the result

We want to make this happen and unit-test the result.

Testing Key Widgets

We proposed a screen design earlier. The first thing we can test is that key widgets are present: a label, a query field, a button, and a table. There may be other components on the panel (for example, subpanels used for organization), but we don't care about them.

So we'll create *testWidgetsPresent()*. To make this work, we need a panel for the overall screen ("SearchPanel"), the label ("searchLabel"), a textfield for entering the query ("queryField"), a button ("findButton"), and a table for the results ("resultTable"). We'll let these widgets be package-access, so our test can see them.

```
public void testWidgetsPresent() {
    SearchPanel panel = new SearchPanel();
    assertNotNull(panel.searchLabel);
    assertNotNull(panel.queryField);
    assertNotNull(panel.findButton);
    assertNotNull(panel.resultTable);
}
```

The test fails to compile. (Of course, we haven't created *SearchPanel* yet.) So create class *SearchPanel* with its widget fields, so we can compile. Don't initialize the widgets yet—run the test and verify that it fails. (It's good practice to see the test fail once; this helps assure you that it captures failures, and lets you ensure that the testing is driving the coding.) Code enough assignments to make the test pass.

Things to notice:

✧ The test helped design the panel's (software) interface.

✧ The test is robust against even dramatic rearrangements of the widgets.

✧ We took very small steps, bouncing between test, code, and design.

✧ Our panel might not (and in fact, does not) actually display anything—we haven't tested that.

✧ The panel still doesn't do anything (for example, if the button were clicked).

We can make another test, to verify that the widgets are set up correctly:

```
public void testInitialContents() {
    SearchPanel sp = new SearchPanel();
    assertEquals("Search:", sp.searchLabel.getText());
    assertEquals("", sp.queryField.getText());
    assertEquals("Find", sp.findButton.getText());
    assert("Table starts empty", sp.resultTable.getRowCount()
            == 0);
}
```

Run this test, and we're OK.
At this point, our *SearchPanel* code looks like this:

```
public class SearchPanel extends JPanel {
    JLabel searchLabel = new JLabel("Search:");
    JTextField queryField = new JTextField();
    JButton findButton = new JButton("Find");
    JTable resultTable = new JTable();

    public SearchPanel() { }
}
```

We could go in either of two directions: push on developing the user interface or its interconnection with searching. The urge to "see" the interface is strong, but we'll resist it in favor of interconnection.

Testing Interconnection

Somehow we must associate a Searcher with our GUI, and verify that we display its results.

We'll give our panel two methods, *getSearcher()* and *setSearcher()*, that will associate a Searcher with the panel. This decision lets us write another test:

```
public void testSearcherSetup() {
    Searcher s = new Searcher() {
        public Result search(Query q) {return null;}
    };

    SearchPanel panel = new SearchPanel();
    assert ("Searcher not set", panel.getSearcher() != s);
    panel.setSearcher(s);
    assert("Searcher now set", panel.getSearcher() == s);
}
```

The compile fails, so bounce over to the *SearchPanel*, add the methods, run the tests again, and they fail. Implement the set/get methods, and the test passes.

The panel still can't do much, but now we can associate a Searcher with it.

Testing with a Fake Searcher

A search returns a set of results. When something returns a list of values, I'm always interested to see how it will behave when it returns 0, 1, or an arbitrary number.

Because this is a unit test, I don't want to depend on the real Searcher implementations; I'd rather create my own for testing purposes. This lets me control behavior in a fine-grained way. Here I'll create a new Searcher called *TestSearcher*. We'll have the query string be an integer, which will tell how many items to return. We'll name the items "a0" (for first author), "t1" (second title), and so on.

But first, a test. (Notice this is a test of our testing class, not of our GUI.)

```
public void testTestSearcher() {
    assertEquals(new Query("1").getValue(), "1");

    Document d = new TestDocument(1);
    assertEquals("y1", d.getYear());

    Result tr = new TestResult(2);
    assert(tr.getCount() == 2);
    assertEquals("a0", tr.getItem(0).getAuthor());

    TestSearcher ts = new TestSearcher();
    tr = ts.find(ts.makeQuery("2"));
    assert("Result has 2 items", tr.getCount() == 2);
    assertEquals("y1", tr.getItem(1).getYear());
}
```

We go through the usual compile/fail cycle and create the test classes, starting with *TestDocument*:

```
public class TestDocument implements Document {
    int count;
    public TestDocument(int n) {count = n;}
    public String getAuthor() {return "a" + count;}
```

```
        public String getTitle() {return "t" + count;}
        public String getYear() {return "y" + count;}
    }
```

The *TestResult* class has a constructor that takes an integer telling how many rows should be present:

```
public class TestResult implements Result {
    int count;
    public TestResult(int n) {count = n;}
    public int getCount() {return count;}
    public Document getItem(int i) {
        return new TestDocument(i);}
}
```

TestSearcher uses the number value of the query string to create the result:

```
public class TestSearcher implements Searcher {
    public Result find(Query q) {
        int count = 0;
        try {count = Integer.parseInt(q.getValue());}
        catch (Exception ignored) {}

        return new TestResult(count);
    }
}
```

Run the test again, and it passes.

0, 1, and Many

We'll build tests for the 0, 1, and many cases:

```
public void test0() {
    SearchPanel sp = new SearchPanel();
    sp.setSearcher (new TestSearcher());
    sp.queryField.setText("0");
    sp.findButton.doClick();
    assert("Empty result", sp.resultTable.getRowCount() == 0);
}
```

At last, we're using the GUI: setting text fields, clicking buttons, and so on.

We run the test, and it passes! This means we already have a working solution if our searcher always returns zero items.

We move on:

```
public void test1() {
    SearchPanel sp = new SearchPanel();
    sp.setSearcher (new TestSearcher());
    sp.queryField.setText("1");
    sp.findButton.doClick();

    assert("1-row result", sp.resultTable.getRowCount() == 1);
    assertEquals(
        "a0",
        sp.resultTable.getValueAt(0,0).toString());
}
```

Now we fail because we don't have any event-handling code on the button.

When the button is clicked, we want to form the string in the text field into a query, and let the searcher find us a result we can display in the table. However, we have a problem in matching types: the Searcher gives us a Result, but the table in our GUI needs a *TableModel*. We need an adapter to make the interfaces conform.

Record Our Mental Stack

We have several things in progress at the same time, so it's a good time to review them—and write them down—so we don't lose track of anything.

- ✧ Write the button code
- ✧ Test and develop a *TableModel* adapter
- ✧ Get test1() to pass
- ✧ Write testN() and get it to pass
- ✧ Test the "look" of the GUI

Adapter Implementation

Let's write the button code as if a *ResultTableAdapter* class existed:

```
findButton.addActionListener(new ActionListener() {
    public void actionPerformed(ActionEvent e) {
    Query q = new Query(queryField.getText());
```

```
        resultTable.setModel(
            new ResultTableAdapter(getSearcher().find(q)));
        }
    });
```

When this fails to compile, stub out a dummy implementation:

```
public class ResultTableAdapter extends DefaultTableModel {
    public ResultTableAdapter(Result r) {}
}
```

Test0() still passes, and *test1()* still fails.

The adapter is straightforward to write, but we begin by writing a test.

```
public void testResultTableAdapter() {
    Result result = new TestResult(2);
    ResultTableAdapter rta = new ResultTableAdapter(result);
    assertEquals("Author", rta.getColumnName(0));
    assertEquals("Title", rta.getColumnName(1));
    assertEquals("Year", rta.getColumnName(2));
    assert("3 columns", rta.getColumnCount() == 3);

    assert("Row count=2", rta.getRowCount() == 2);
    assertEquals("a0", rta.getValueAt(0,0).toString());
    assertEquals("y1", rta.getValueAt(1,2).toString());
}
```

The test fails because the dummy implementation doesn't do anything.

Bounce over and implement the *ResultTableAdapter*. Change it to be a subclass of *AbstractTableModel* (instead of *DefaultTableModel*), then implement the column names, column and row counts, and finally *getValueAt()*.

```
public class ResultTableAdapter
        extends AbstractTableModel implements TableModel {
    final static String columnNames[] = {"Author", "Title",
                                          "Year"};
    Result myResult;

    public ResultTableAdapter(Result r) {myResult = r;}

    public String getColumnName(int i) {return columnNames[i];}
```

```
public int getColumnCount() {return columnNames.length;}

public int getRowCount() {return myResult.getItemCount();}

public Object getValueAt(int r, int c) {
    Document doc = myResult.getItem(r);

    switch(c) {
    case 0: return doc.getAuthor();
    case 1: return doc.getTitle();
    case 2: return doc.getYear();
    default: return "?";
    }
    }
}
```

This test (*testResultTableAdapter*) should pass, and so should test1().

TestN and More

Write *testN()*, with, say, five items. It will also pass.

What else can give you problems? One possible problem occurs when we do a sequence of queries—can we get "leftovers"? For example, a query returning five items followed by a query returning three items should have only three items in the table. (If the table were improperly cleared, we might see the last two items of the previous query.)

We can test a sequence of queries:

```
public void testQuerySequenceForLeftovers() {
    SearchPanel sp = new SearchPanel();
    sp.setSearcher (new TestSearcher());

    sp.queryField.setText("5");
    sp.findButton.doClick();
    assert(sp.resultTable.getRowCount() == 5);

    sp.queryField.setText("3");
    sp.findButton.doClick();
    assert(sp.resultTable.getRowCount() == 3);
}
```

This test passes.

Testing for Looks

We have a properly connected panel. We can check the widgets' relative locations:

- ❖ label left-of *queryField*
- ❖ *queryField* left-of findButton
- ❖ *queryField* above table

(Would we bother with these tests? Perhaps not, we might just put the panel on-screen and deal with its contents manually. There are times when such tests would definitely be appropriate, such as when we're working against a style guide or when the window format is expected to be stable.)

To make this test run, we need to put our panel in a frame or window. (Components don't have their screen locations set until their containing window is created.)

```
public void testRelativePosition() {
    SearchPanel sp = new SearchPanel();

    JFrame display = new JFrame("test");
    display.getContentPane().add(sp);
    display.setSize(500,500);
    display.setVisible(true);

    //try {Thread.sleep(3000);} catch (Exception ex) {}

    assert ("label left-of query",
        sp.searchLabel.getLocationOnScreen().x
      < sp.queryField.getLocationOnScreen().x);

    assert ("query left-of button",
        sp.queryField.getLocationOnScreen().x
      < sp.findButton.getLocationOnScreen().x);

    assert ("query above table",
        sp.queryField.getLocationOnScreen().y
      < sp.resultTable.getLocationOnScreen().y);
}
```

The test fails, as we haven't done anything to put widgets on the panel. (You can uncomment the *sleep()* if you want to see it on-screen.)

To implement panels, I usually do a screen design that shows the intermediate panels and layouts:

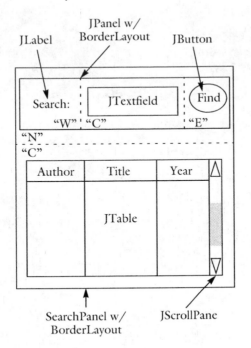

Now we can lay out the panel:

```
public SearchPanel() {
    super (new BorderLayout());

    findButton.addActionListener(new ActionListener() {
        public void actionPerformed(ActionEvent e) {
            Query q = new Query(queryField.getText());
            resultTable.setModel(
                new ResultTableAdapter(getSearcher().find(q)));
        }
    });
    JPanel topPanel = new JPanel(new BorderLayout());
    topPanel.add(searchLabel, BorderLayout.WEST);
    topPanel.add(queryField, BorderLayout.CENTER);
    topPanel.add(findButton, BorderLayout.EAST);

    this.add(topPanel, BorderLayout.NORTH);
    this.add(new JScrollPane(resultTable),
            BorderLayout.CENTER);
}
```

Compile, test, and it works.

We've successfully implemented our panel!

Main

To complete the system, we'll create a *main()* routine:

```
public class Main {
    public static void main(String[] args) {
        if (args.length == 0) {
            System.err.println(
                "Arg-file w/tab-delimited author/title/year");
            System.exit(1);
        }

        Searcher searcher = null;
        try {
            searcher = SearcherFactory.get(args[0]);
        } catch (Exception ex) {
            System.err.println(
                "Unable to open file " + args[0] + "; " + ex);
            System.exit(1);
        }

        SearchPanel sp = new SearchPanel();
        sp.setSearcher(searcher);

        JFrame display = new JFrame("Bibliographic System-"
                                    + args[0]);
        display.getContentPane().add(sp);
        display.setSize(500,500);
        display.setVisible(true);
    }
}
```

Conclusions

We've completed development of our user interface. Not every aspect of a GUI can be unit-tested through the approach we've used, but we've identified a number of useful techniques:

- ✧ Even GUI development can maintain the cycle-in-the-small of test-code design.
- ✧ GUI tests can be robust against changes in how the widgets are arranged on-screen.

- Fields and buttons can be simulated with *getText()*, *setText()*, *doClick()*, and so on.
- Stub out the services provided by the model to get fine-grained control over what the GUI test shows.
- We can test relative positioning using *getLocationOnScreen()*.

Unit tests can be tedious to write, but they save you time in the future (by catching bugs after changes). Less obvious, but just as important, is that they can save you time now: tests focus your design and implementation on simplicity, they support refactoring, and they validate features as you develop.

Resources
- Code for this example can be found on http://users.vnet.net/wwake.
- *The Test/Code Cycle in XP: Part 1, Model*, William Wake,[1] found on http://users.vnet.net/wwake.
- *Extreme Programming Explained*, Kent Beck.
- *Refactoring*, Martin Fowler.
- JUnit can be found on http://www.XProgramming.com.

---

1. Copyright 2000, William C. Wake, used with permission. William .Wake@acm.org.

Chapter 32

A True Story

Ron Jeffries [re]learns something about simplicity.

We are writing this book using Adobe FrameMaker. Frame, as we affectionately call it, lets us store the chapters in individual files and organize them into a book in a separate book file. It turns out that we could use a little extra automation of our work, so I thought I'd just code up a little application. I wrote a few stories—here are a couple:

- Report which files in the book directory aren't actually used in the book file. Ignore the backup files.
- After adding and updating chapters, send just the files that have changed to Chet and Ann.

We're in the midst of a fairly large reordering of chapters, and I really wanted the list of files that exist but aren't in the book. Last night I set out to implement that story in Dolphin Smalltalk. (Don't worry, I'm not going to make you read the code.)

It turns out that Dolphin doesn't have an object that represents a file directory or folder. Instead, it can give you a list of "file specs" that match a pattern. Well, obviously I'm going to need a Directory object, so I started on it last night. I wrote some tests, some code, and got a decent start at it. I put a few hours into it, and it was a bit harder than I thought, and I hadn't even gotten to the idea of a Directory holding another Directory. So I posted a question on the Dolphin newsgroup, and went to bed.

This morning I still wanted the list of files that weren't in the book, but I had come to my senses. The value was in that list of files, not some general support for directories. I went back to the story: report which files in the book directory aren't in the book file.

I created a test for a "*BookAnalyzer*" object. The test checked to see if the analyzer could learn which files were used. This was easy, as there's a script from Frame that writes that information out to a text file. That test was running in no time.

Then I wrote a test that asks the *BookAnalyzer* for the *unused files*. I implemented that by intention, by asking for the chapter files and removing all the used files. I implemented the chapter files by asking for the *.fm* files and removing all the backup.fm files. I implemented the *.fm* files by getting the list of file specs from the book directory that matched *.fm*.

Well, guess what? Done in an hour, works perfectly, and doesn't need a Directory object at all.

I put a couple of chapters in that had been missed, deleted a couple of files that were no longer relevant, and got on with business.

Now in microcosm there are some important lessons here, lessons I need to relearn time and again:

- ✧ I was working alone. A partner might have kept me from starting. Surely a partner would have gotten bored with messing with Directory for so long.
- ✧ Small releases provide immediate business value. I got and used the information I really needed with my small project this morning.
- ✧ Simple solutions are faster. The *BookAnalyzer* got done in half the time I put into Directory, which still isn't done.

You might have one major concern—didn't I wind up with some very specialized and hacked together code, instead of the Directory object I will really need someday?

I don't think so. The file name manipulation in *BookAnalyzer* is clean, clear, and all in separate methods. As I generally do, I finished up the object by making sure it used good names and was generally well factored.

The next time I need to do some directory-like stuff, I'll go to that code, pull it out into a little object, enhance it if needed, and use it in *BookAnalyzer* and for the new task. If a Directory object turns out to be what I really need, I'm sure I'll evolve to it easily. More likely I'll get something better, and more useful for what I really need to do.

What we have here is a small example of why we say to do the simplest thing that could possibly work. Take it to heart. Try working this way for a while. We're sure it will work for you, too.

Chapter 33

Estimates
and Promises

*We **estimate** how long the project will take. We **promise** to tell the truth about how we're doing.*

We believe, and therefore teach, that we cannot know how long it will take to do software we've never done before. Therefore, we cannot, with integrity, promise exactly what will be done. What we can do is estimate what will be done, and promise to do our best and to tell the truth about what happens.

No one really knows how long the project will take. The very best ways of finding out only result in estimates. If we were to break the project down into tiny tasks each of which was obvious, and arrange them in a PERT chart with a complete contingency analysis, and did everything we could think of like that, what we would wind up with would be a very complex estimate. The first snow day or the flu could make a mockery of our plan. Something will make a mockery of any such plan.

Therefore, all planning processes have mechanisms for dealing with the uncertainties. They produce a range of results, perhaps, or they fudge the result by multiplying all the estimates by 3.14.

It is just not possible to promise, with integrity, to be finished exactly on any given day with exactly this much work done. We don't mean that it's hard; we mean that it is not possible. And we value integrity.

Much of the pain of software development revolves around a simple error: mistaking an estimate for a promise.

Here's what programmers can promise and what the practices in this book will help deliver:

1. You can promise to estimate the difficulty of the entire project, each story in the project, and each task in each story, as accurately as you can.
2. You can promise to track those estimates to improve your ability to know how hard things are going to be.
3. You can promise to track delivery performance, to make it clear how fast the project is really going.
4. You can promise to use the facts to refine the picture of when the project will be done, by estimating again as you learn, and by using the velocity so far to predict where you'll be by any given date, or to predict the date when you'll have chosen features done.

Estimate the Entire Project as Accurately as Possible

Estimate the project by breaking it down into "stories" that are small enough to understand and to estimate in week-sized chunks.

Estimate the stories by breaking them down into "tasks" that are small enough to understand and to estimate in day-sized chunks.

Estimate the tasks one at a time, and watch your performance to improve your accuracy.

Track Estimates to Get Project Velocity

Divide implementation into short periods called iterations, and keep track of how many stories you get done in each iteration. The pace at which you currently develop stories is an excellent predictor of your future pace.

Track the tasks you do in each iteration, and note how long each one takes compared to how long you expected. This gives you an even better predictor of your day-to-day ability to implement tasks. Since you can estimate tasks better and better, and since stories are made up of tasks, you will learn to estimate stories better as you go.

Refine the Picture

With improving ability to predict everyday progress, and improving ability to relate past stories to future ones, you can easily improve your estimates.

The improved estimates do come closer to promises, but an XP team doesn't fall into that trap. They know that estimates are just guesses wearing a nice outfit. Instead, the XP team uses actual performance, plus enhanced estimates, to control the project outcome.

Control the Outcome

If you know how fast you are going and you know when you need to be done, you can do an excellent job of selecting what to do to get the best possible program by that date. You do this by selecting the essential stories first, then the very valuable ones, then the less valuable ones, and so on.

If you have a critical release date, expect that you will have to make some choices of what to leave out. And remember—that's a good thing, because so many projects deliver less than you asked for without letting you choose what you get.

Because an XP team can give you good estimates of how hard each story is to do and can give good reports of how long such things take, you can make your project a success in spite of the fact that no one really knows exactly how long the project will take.

Chapter 34

Everything That
Could Possibly Break

*Test everything that could possibly break. What does this mean?
How is it possible?*

In XP, programmers write unit tests for all their code. The rule is: Test everything that could possibly break.

Sometimes people get really angry at us when we talk about this rule. "Don't you know it's impossible to prove that a program works by testing," they'll shout. "Don't you know an infinite number of things could go wrong?"

Yes, your authors took those courses and read those papers, too. Hold your horses, as people used to say in Jeffries's day, and hear us out.

First of all, like all the XP rules, this one is meant to make us think, and to keep us on the hook. In XP, we turn all the dials up to ten, not up to Reasonable.

Test everything that could possibly break. As we test, this impossible banner waves over our head. As we abandon testing an object, we ask ourselves seriously whether we have tested everything about it that could possible break. Because we're realists, we stop before writing an infinite number of tests. But we try hard to test everything that could possibly break.

Sometimes, because we're human, a defect slips through. When that happens, we note that something broke, and that it wasn't tested. Oops, fell short. Well, we knew it was impossible, so we don't feel too bad. But let's take a moment to learn from what happened. Maybe we can't test everything, but we sure want to test everything that is going to break, and this thing here just broke. We needed a test.

So we *Test to show a defect,* and while we're at it, we make some notes and write a few more tests, whatever this mistake reminds us of.

But wait, don't answer yet. There's more! If you go back and see what is really being said in those famous old theories, it's that it's not possible to test any sufficiently complex program. Those theories always show the exponentially increasing number of branches and paths through the system, and they whine about how you couldn't possibly test them all.

This is all true. The more complex an object is, the harder it is to test it completely. But the reverse is also true: the simpler an object or method is, the easier it is to test.

When we are testing some object and we can see things that might break, but they seem impossible to test, we let the pressure to test everything that could break flow back into the design. Maybe we can simplify this object, break it up, and make it easier to test.

It turns out that usually we can simplify the code and make it easier to test. In the process, we make the code easier to understand, and easier to get right. It's a win all around. We get better code and better testing.

Try to test everything that could possibly break. You'll be glad you did.

Does This Mean to Test Every Object and Every Method?

The rule is to test everything that could possibly break. To save time, don't test things that couldn't possibly break. There are more things that couldn't possibly break than you might imagine.

Start conservatively on identifying things not to test. Until you're sure, test. But unit testing is "white box" testing. You look at the code when you write the test, and if the code can't break, then don't test it.

Accessors can't break. There's no need to test them. Unless, of course, you have a tendency to forget to write them, and no other test is going to find that they're missing. But wait—if no other test is going to access them, they shouldn't be there anyway. So probably you don't need to test accessors.

Even if it's more complex, sometimes code just can't break. Here's an example in Smalltalk:

```
printAccounts
    accounts do: [ :each | each print]
```

That method loops over the collection named *accounts,* and tells each account to *print.* The method can't possibly break. There are other things that could break: *accounts* might not be a collection, and, depending on the code, you might need to test that. *Accounts* might not know how to print themselves, or their printing might break. You might need to test that. But, in my opinion, you don't need to test the *printAccounts* method. (Just my luck there'll be a bug in it. Well, live and learn.)

I (Jeffries here) used to teach that if an object was used extensively in other objects, maybe you didn't need to test it directly. I'm not so sure anymore. Just the other day, looking at a client's code, I found an object that needed some work to be really good code. I grabbed a partner and we sat down to work. First thing we noticed was that the object wasn't directly tested. It was exercised rather fully by the test for another object, but when we got to refactoring the first object, it didn't seem that those tests were correctly aimed. So we wrote some tests, then refactored. It went very smoothly. And I learned a lesson: it's better if every class has its own tests.

That same day I was browsing the code, as I do when I stop by to visit, and I found a method that couldn't possibly work. I mean it could not possibly work. There was an if statement in it, and one of the branches answered a different kind of object from the other branch. Sure enough, there were no tests for that branch of the if. The right thing to do might have been to write a test and then fix the method. In fact, however, when we looked at the users of the method, no one was using the object in a way that could ever invoke that branch of the if statement. So we removed the feature instead of writing the test.

My general recommendation now is that any nontrivial object needs tests. By nontrivial I mean any object that has behavior. Maybe you don't need to test record objects, objects with nothing but accessors. I still wouldn't test every method. I'd skip methods that couldn't possibly break. And I'd let my experience with defects found outside the object's own tests guide me in understanding when things couldn't possibly break.

Test Everything Example

Regarding our rule, *Test everything that could possibly break,* a correspondent wrote to Ron:

> *"Everything" means just that, right? Software can do lots of desirable and undesirable things, and XP is supposed to test for everything.*
>
> *That strikes me as either impossible (number of execution cycles approaches infinity) or vague (we know the previous, so we test for almost everything or some other such subset).*

Here's a short example of how we would test an object. We'll do the thing in Smalltalk because we can do it faster. We'll comment the code for folks who don't know Smalltalk very well. We're sure you'll do fine.

The task is to build a class named *Account* that holds collections of transactions and that can answer the balance of the transactions.

Transactions, by hypothesis, already exist. We have a simple *Transaction* class, so far, that just holds positive deposits and negative withdrawals:

```
Object subclass: #Transaction
    instanceVariableNames: 'amount'
    classVariableNames: ''
    poolDictionaries: ''!

!Transaction methodsFor!
setAmount: anAmount
    amount := anAmount!

value
    ^amount! !

!Transaction class methodsFor!

deposit: anAmount
    "A deposit is a Transaction with a positive amount"
    ^self new setAmount: anAmount!

withdraw: anAmount
    "A withdrawal is a Transaction with a negative amount"
    ^self new setAmount: anAmount negated! !
```

We have written two tests, one that checks an *Account* with no entries (written mostly because it was the simplest test that we could think of), and one that checks an *Account* with three entries:

```
TestCase subclass: #AccountTest
    instanceVariableNames: ''
    classVariableNames: ''
    poolDictionaries: ''!

!AccountTest methodsFor!

testEmpty
    self should: [Account new balance = 0]!

testThree
    | account |
    account := Account new.
    account add: (Transaction deposit: 100).
    account add: (Transaction withdraw: 15).
    account add: (Transaction withdraw: 25).
    self should: [account balance = 60].! !
```

Finally, here's the `Account` class as we have presently implemented it. We'll comment a bit more fully on each method:

```
Object subclass: #Account
    instanceVariableNames: 'transactions'
    classVariableNames: ''
    poolDictionaries: ''!
```

The class contains transactions. We'll see below that these are an *OrderedCollection* (similar to Java Vector).

```
add: aTransaction
    self transactions add: aTransaction!
```

This method gets the transactions collection (see below) and adds the method parameter, *aTransaction,* to the collection. The method `add:` is standard behavior on *OrderedCollections,* and can add anything at all to the collection.

```
balance
    ^self transactions
        inject: 0
        into: [ :sum :each | sum + each value]!
```

The *inject:into:* method on collections initializes `sum` with the input value (in this case zero), and executes the *into:* block once per element of the collection. This is a standard Smalltalk idiom for adding things up.

This particular usage takes the transaction collection and sums whatever it gets by sending `value` to each Transaction. (We happen to know that this will be a positive number for a deposit and a negative number for a withdrawal.)

```
transactions
    transactions isNil ifTrue:
        [transactions := OrderedCollection new].
    ^transactions! !
```

This method checks to see if the `transactions` instance variable is *nil,* which it is guaranteed to be for a new instance. If it is *nil,* it is initialized to be an empty *OrderedCollection.* Then the instance variable, now guaranteed to be an *OrderedCollection,* is answered.

Now then. We want to assert that for our new class, `Account`, we have tested everything that could possibly break. Hold your objections regarding the *Transaction* class and the system as a whole for a moment. Let's just talk about `Account`. What else could break?

Transactions that don't answer numbers when sent `value` could blow up the system, but the error would not be in this class. (Some people would suggest asserting that *aTransaction* is a Transaction, or that it supports some interface. That would address system integrity, but it would not increase the correctness of the code we have, in our opinion.)

We honestly can't think of what else could break. *OrderedCollections* work as does the `add:` variable. The code clearly inits the variable `transactions` once and only once.

So, have we tested everything that could possibly break on our class Account? We think so.

Now then. We have not shown the tests for *Transaction*. Would they be hard to write? Probably not. The big question is whether we should check integrity for the amounts, determining that they're numeric. Again, not our job in the style we advocate, but in Eiffel you'd certainly be tempted. Since *Transaction* has essentially no behavior, it's not hard to test.

That leaves us with the system problems like "What if someone creates a non-transaction and sends it to an account?" Well now. Any class that (thinks it) is creating *Transactions* and putting them in *Accounts* must have a test. Would it be hard to test? We don't know, but our rule is that we must test everything about it that could possibly break. If the code visibly started with numbers and created *Transactions* with *deposit:* and *withdraw:*, it would probably be pretty clear how much to test it.

So we feel that sure that when it is time to test the *AccountBuilder*, we'll again find it easy to test everything that could possibly break.

And, finally, remember that there are *acceptance tests* as well. These are designed to test whether the system, in actual use, ever gets wrong answers or blows up. If/when these tests found something, they would point, almost inevitably, to a particular class (like *Account-Builder*) that was doing something wrong, that is, that wasn't tested enough. We would learn something about what to test in such classes, add the necessary test(s), and add similar tests everywhere we thought we needed them.

In no case, it seems to me, are we likely to run into combinatorial problems, problems of writing an infinite number of tests, or such. There's just no place for them to happen; wherever we invoke them, we are writing a class, and that class can support a sensible and quite finite collection of tests.

Now, of course, this is just a simple example. But in my strong opinion, it is not at all atypical. Most everything one ever needs to do can be built this simply and incrementally and can be tested. None of us always does it, but each of us nearly always could, and would benefit if we did.

Questions About the Example

One of our favorite reviewers wasn't so sure we had tested everything. He asked:

Can the Account Go Negative? How Negative?

Yes, clearly it can, because the `balance` method just adds up the transactions, without regard to their sign. Does that need a unit test? Not in my opinion, because it can't possibly break.

Does it need an acceptance test? Almost certainly.

Can an Account Have Fractions Less than One Penny?

The code doesn't say. What will determine the answer will be the class of the object that comes back from sending `value` to a *Transaction*. That might be something as simple as an *Integer* or a *Float*, but it is more likely some kind of monetary type. In any case, the answer isn't here in *Account*, but in that class.

Is There a Maximum Size on the Account?

Our reviewer might have meant maximum number of *Transactions* or maximum balance, but we're not sure which.

The *transactions* variable is initialized to an *OrderedCollection*. In Smalltalk, these have no maximum size. So there is no maximum number of *Transactions*.

The maximum `balance` value will depend on the underlying numeric type of the `value` field of a *Transaction*. In Smalltalk, the built-in numeric types have no limit—they can get as large as they want. If there is a test for this at all, it would be in the monetary type that's inside the `Transaction`.

Summary Response to the Review Questions

The authors would stick with the tests, in the example, and feel that they have tested everything that could possibly break in the *Account* class. With similar diligence in *Transaction* and the monetary classes, they'd feel very confident overall.

Other testers might test more or less. It always comes down to one's best professional judgment in the specific case: have I tested everything that could possibly break in this code?

Afterword

I have been looking at XP for a while and have talked to a lot of people (including Ron Jeffries and Kent Beck) about it. And I think that a lot of us are missing the point of why XP works. Quite simply, I think that XP works because it is validation-centric rather than product-centric. "Huh?" you say.

First, what do I mean by *validation* and *production*? Well, production is the act of actually constructing some product, and validation is the act of assuring that this product actually does what it is supposed to do.

Typically, validation means that somebody other than the producer analyzes the product and assures that it satisfies its purpose. Now, on with the discussion.

When you are developing any software system, two questions must be answered:

- ✧ Are we developing the right software?
- ✧ Are we developing the software right?

Essentially, the first question is about analysis (What is it supposed to do?) and validation (Does it actually do it?), and the second question is about design and construction (Is this the right architecture? Does it satisfy the "ilities"?). Can you say inception/transition versus elaboration/construction? I knew you could.

We also know that the first question is much more important than the second, since developing the wrong software right is useless. So, because XP does everything to extremes, we would expect it to focus on the first question to the exclusion of the second. Almost, but not quite.

So what does XP do to address the first question? In my opinion, everything except refactoring (and only half of that). This is because the essence of validation is communication, and almost everything about XP is to facilitate communication: between the customer and developer and between developers.

And because XP is extreme, it only wants face-to-face communication: pair programming, planning, and so on. And it insists on a second pair of eyes on everything. It's all about validating everything that is done, all the time.

As far as I can tell, the main thing about XP that is not all about either easing communications or developing the right system is refactoring (although refactoring is partly about establishing clearer communication of what the code does). It is clear that refactoring is a good thing to do, and, since XP is extreme, if a little refactoring is good, XP insists on total refactoring. Refactoring is the thing that allows architecture to emerge from the code, and this emergent architecture is what allows ease of maintenance, extensibility, and so on—that is, it allows us to answer the second question.

I hear you ask, "So what, Dan? Is this a useful message you're giving me or just random ramblings?"

Good question. A little of both, I think. Let's compare XP to what we usually do. In most processes we have a list of products (models, documents, code, and so on) to produce, and processes to use to produce and validate them. So far, so good. In the crunch, unfortunately, our focus always becomes the production of products rather than the validation of them. This is because most processes are product-centric, and I believe this is because management can measure production, but not validation.

XP won't allow this to happen. If you're not validating everything all the time, you're not doing XP. Period. By the way, this is why the concepts of XP are so tantalizing to me. It is not the lack of ceremony, nor is it how happy the developers are; it is that everything is validated all the time. Very cool.

My belief is that XP is the first popular process with this focus on validation built in. It won't be the last. I hope.

—Dan Rawsthorne, Ph.D.
Director of Program Management and Development Practices
ACCESS, a communications company
DrDan@dsign.com
http://www.dsign.com/

Annotated Bibliography

The purpose of this section is to give you a chance to dig deeper into the aspects of XP that interest you, and to see some of the aspects of life that have brought the authors to this point.

Scott Adams, *The Dilbert Principle*, HarperCollins, 1996; ISBN 0887307876.

> Bill Rogers, Ron's old mentor, always used to say, "You have to either laugh or cry." Join Scott Adams and Dilbert, and laugh.

Robert C. Atkins, M.D., *Dr. Atkins' New Diet Revolution*, Avon Books, 1999; ISBN 0380803682.

> Don't ask.

Kent Beck, *Extreme Programming Explained*, Addison-Wesley, 2000, ISBN 0201616416.

> The book that started XP happening. We are pleased to have been there while it happened. Thank you, Kent.

Kent Beck, *Smalltalk Best Practice Patterns*, Prentice-Hall, 1996; ISBN 013476904X.

> For Smalltalk programmers, you can do no better than to follow these patterns for writing clear, consistent, and communicative code. Need a coding standard? Use this one.

Boris Beizer, *Black-Box Testing*, John Wiley and Sons, 1995; ISBN 0471120944.

> Beizer hopes "that for most of us, testing ceases to be a profession, but an inseparable aspect of what every conscientious developer routinely does."

David Bellin and Susan Suchman Simone, *The CRC Card Book*, Addison-Wesley, 1997; ISBN 0201895358.

> Bellin and Simone take CRC where it has never gone before. Good material on brainstorming, requirements gathering, and collaboration. Even some implementation.

Jon Louis Bentley, *Programming Pearls, Second Edition* Addison-Wesley, 1999; ISBN 0201657880.

> Pearls, indeed. This collection of columns from Bentley's column in CACM addresses things you need to know in simple, clear language.

Ambrose Bierce, *The Devil's Dictionary*, Dover Publications, 1958 (original publication 1911).

> "Hope, *n*. Desire and expectation rolled into one." The original and in many ways still the best.

Robert V. Binder, *Testing Object-Oriented Systems*, Addison-Wesley, 2000, ISBN 0201809389.

> Binder provides almost 1,200 pages on testing. Every technique you could need, and many you could not, are in this book. Strive to write programs such that you will need only to scratch the surface. No XP-scale program should ever need all this. But it's here if you do need it.

Kenneth Blanchard, Ph.D., and Spencer Johnson, Ph.D., *The One-Minute Manager*, Berkeley Books, 1982; ISBN 0425098478.

> Be present. Delegate. Follow up.

Barry W. Boehm, *Software Engineering Economics*, Prentice Hall, 1981; ISBN 0138221227.

> In the range of the economics curve where the cost of change is nearly flat, XP recommends deferring unnecessary investment. This

very expensive book is the only resource we know for using economics in software decision-making. Check it at the library to see if you need a copy.

Grady Booch, *Object-Oriented Analysis and Design with Applications, Second Edition,* Addison-Wesley, 1994; ISBN 0805353402.

Notationally dated, this book talks about real applications and how they might be designed with objects. We still look at it from time to time.

Daniel J. Boorstin, *The Creators: A History of Heroes of the Imagination,* Vintage Books, 1992; ISBN 0679743758.

How "Man-the Creator" built Western civilization by imagining it.

Frederick P. Brooks, Jr., *The Mythical Man-Month, Anniversary Edition,* Addison-Wesley, 1995; ISBN 0201835959.

The anniversary edition of the original, published in 1975. Brooks was one of the first to address programming as a people business and a management business, not just a technical business.

Dan Carrison and Rod Walsh, *Semper Fi,* Business Leadership the Marine Corps Way, American Management Association, 1999; ISBN 0814404138.

You think not? Think again. What about recruiting the best, communicating clearly, leading with integrity, accepting responsibility?

Lewis Carroll, Introduction and Notes by Martin Gardner, *The Annotated Alice,* World Publishing Company, 1963.

The complete text of *Wonderland* and *Looking Glass,* annotated by the famous author of *Mathematical Recreations* in *Scientific American.* If you love Alice, find a copy of this book.

Clayton M. Christensen, *The Innovator's Dilemma,* Harvard Business School Press, 1997; ISBN 0875845851.

XP is about how to build the value that the business people ask for. *The Innovator's Dilemma* addresses how disruptive new technologies can throw successful companies into failure. Not a license to program what you're not asked for, but a license to ask good questions.

Alistair Cockburn, *Surviving Object-Oriented Projects, A Manager's Guide,* Addison-Wesley, 1998; ISBN 0201498340.

> Alistair is a project anthropologist. He has visited many projects, observing not just what they say, but what they really do. From this experience, he provides guidance and suggestions for your projects. Alistair favors a light approach to projects. The book is worth it for the pullout checklist alone, but it has much much more!

James C. Collins and Jerry I. Porras, *Built to Last*, HarperCollins, 1997; ISBN 0887307396.

> What makes great companies great? Collins and Porras studied 18 "visionary" corporations, with an eye to what makes them truly different. If you must be in a large company, these are the kind you'd like to be in.

Daryl R. Conner, *Leading at the Edge of Chaos*, John Wiley and Sons, 1998; ISBN 0471295574.

Daryl R. Conner, *Managing at the Speed of Change*, Villard, 1992; ISBN 0679406840.

> Conner sees his job as "leading people through the jungle of change." With its focus on embracing change, XP is one tool for dealing with the need for rapid change in information systems.

Larry L. Constantine, *Constantine on Peopleware*, Yourdon Press, 1995; ISBN 0133319768.

> Larry presents over 30 essays and articles on the people side of software, and of life. He is a practitioner, a theorist, and a top observer of the field.

The Editors of *Cook's Illustrated, The Best Recipe,* Boston Common Press, 1999; ISBN 0936184388

> "Would you make 38 versions of Creme Caramel to find the absolute best version? We did. Here are 700 exhaustively tested recipes plus no-nonsense kitchen tests and tastings." Here is the best cookbook I have seen. They really did try 38 different Creme Caramel recipes and explained which one was best and why.

Mihaly Csikszentmihalyi, *Flow*, Harper Collins, 1990; ISBN 0060920432.

> In our terms, flow is Perfect Engineering Time. Yes, it is possible to attain flow when working in pairs. Lasts longer, too. Here's the definitive work on what flow really is.

Alan M. Davis, *201 Principles of Software Development*, McGraw-Hill, Inc., 1995; ISBN 0070158401.

> This book is a "reader's digest" of some of the classic software engineering references.

Tom DeMarco, *The Deadline*, Dorset House, 1997; ISBN 0932633390.

> A fascinating novel about software project management. Who are the thinly disguised people Tom includes? Does he really believe the things they espouse? This one is entertaining and it will make you think.

Tom Demarco and Timothy Lister, *Peopleware: Productive Projects and Teams*, Second Edition, Dorset House, 1999; ISBN 0932633439.

Tom DeMarco, *Why Does Software Cost So Much?*, Dorset House, 1995; ISBN 093263334X.

> This book of essays covers a lot of issues, and they're all interesting and enjoyable. Tom's angle on managing the software process is light-handed and collaborative. Again, he was there first.

Max Depree, *Leadership Is an Art*, Dell Books, 1990; ISBN 0440503248.

> This book is easy to read, with good advice for both leaders and aspiring leaders.

Edward Dijkstra, *A Discipline of Programming*, Prentice-Hall, 1976; ISBN 013215871X.

> Dijkstra blends the mathematician's view with the programming view. Almost alone, this book started Ron on his lifelong quest for simple and elegant expression in programming.

Barrie Dolnick, *The Executive Mystic: Intuitive Tools for Cultivating the Winning Edge in Business*, HarperCollins Publishers, 1999; ISBN 0887309542.

> Ron got this confused with *The Corporate Mystic*. Both books are worth reading, but they are completely different. So when Ron was explaining what he got out of the book, it was quite humorous.

Bruce Eckel, *Thinking in Java*, Prentice Hall, 1998; ISBN 0136597238.

> Bruce brings a joy and simplicity to his description of Java, moving the reader along the way to thinking in Java. Bruce is also the author of *Thinking in C++*.

Carlton Egremont III, *Mr. Bunny's Big Cup o' Java*, Addison-Wesley, 1999; ISBN 0201615630.

> A humorous look at Java and its programmers. As Smalltalkers, we found it almost enough to make Java tolerable. But take our word for it; it's a fun read. This is not a technical book.

Emily Eisele, *You Don't Eat Spiders,* not yet published, 1996.

> A common sense look at the complexities of life in the postmodern world.

Daniel D. Ferry and Noelle Frances Ferry, *77 Sure-fire Ways to Kill a Software Project*, Buy Books on the web.com, 1999; ISBN 0741400103.

> By thinking, "What could we do to really screw this up?" the Ferrys provide a delightful yet terrifying reminder of most every mistake possible in the software business. Well, 77 of them, anyway. Short, fun, and scary.

Richard P. Feynman, *Surely You're Joking, Mr. Feynman!*, W. W. Norton, 1985, ISBN 0393316041.

> Biographical essays from one of the world's most brilliant and bizarre men.

Martin Fowler, *Analysis Patterns*, Addison-Wesley, 1996; ISBN 0201895420.

> Business design patterns, nearly all you could ever need. Please, start with the simplest ones—but do start here. Gamma, et al. cov-

ered the patterns that make our programs work. Martin covers the patterns that make them accomplish something.

Martin Fowler, *Refactoring: Improving the Design of Existing Code*, Addison-Wesley, 1999; ISBN 0201485672.

> The programming side of XP is all about being ready for the next requirement; refactoring is how you do it. Martin catalogs over 70 refactorings, the key steps in transforming a program to improve its structure while preserving its function. Refactoring is a core practice in XP, and this is the text.

Martin Fowler, *UML Distilled, Second Edition: A Brief Guide to the Standard Object Modeling Language* (The Addison-Wesley Object Technology Series), Addison-Wesley, 1999; ISBN 020165783X.

> In this excellent small volume, Martin captures everything you're ever likely to need to know about UML, except for one key fact: UML diagrams should only be drawn on scrap paper—use them to focus your mind; then embody them in the program.

Daniel P. Freedman, Gerald M. Weinberg, *Handbook of Walkthroughs, Inspections, and Technical Reviews*, Dorset House, 1990; ISBN 0932633196.

> XP's pair programming obviates the need for most inspections and reviews. If you must do them, do them right. Freedman tells you how.

Jack Fultz, *The Comet's Tale, a History.* Self published.

> A history of Chet's hometown as told through its high school athletics. Written by Chet's uncle.

Erich Gamma, Richard Helms, Ralph Johnson, and John Vlissides, *Design Patterns, Elements of Reusable Object-Oriented Software*, Addison-Wesley, 1995; ISBN 0201633612.

> A collection of key design patterns, providing descriptions of problem and solution. These patterns now serve as the official terminology for these ideas. Know them and use them in your designs. If you can't quote from this one, your computer geek friends will make fun of you.

Roger Garrett, *Starship Simulation*, Dilithium Press, 1978; ISBN 091839810X. Out of print.

> Designing and implementing a simulation of a starship on a personal computer. We want to play this game!

Donald C. Gause and Gerald M. Weinberg, *Are Your Lights On?: How to Figure Out What the Problem Really Is*, Dorset House, 1990; ISBN 0932633161.

> This is a fun book about problem-solving and creativity.

Thomas Gilb, et al., *Principles of Software Engineering Management*, Addison-Wesley, 1988; ISBN 0201192462.

> Tom Gilb is very much into incremental development, and measurement. Check him out!

Malcom Gladwell, *The Tipping Point*, Little, Brown, 2000; ISBN 0316316962.

> How do fashion trends come to be? How are unknown books transformed into best-sellers? How do software development processes become used worldwide, making the universe safe for programmers? Gladwell tells us of Connectors, Mavens, Salesmen, and the Stickiness Factor. Does XP have all those? We hope so.

James Gleick, *Genius: The Life and Science of Richard Feynman*, Pantheon, 1992; ISBN 0679747044.

> The story of one of the great minds of the twentieth century. The man who used a spike solution to discover why the shuttle *Challenger* exploded.

Adele Goldberg and David Robson, *Smalltalk-80: The Language*, Addison-Wesley, 1989; ISBN 0201136880.

> If you use Smalltalk, you know the purple book. If you are just wondering why we won't let it go, here is the bible.

Stephen Jay Gould, *The Mismeasure of Man*, Norton, 1996; ISBN 0393314251.

> Science has spent the last 150 years trying to measure human intelligence by using everything from the volume of our skulls to our ability to fill in little circles with a number two pencil. An important lesson for all of us who want to measure performance.

David Halberstam, *The Reckoning,* Morrow, 1986; ISBN 0688048382. Out of print.

> United States versus Japan, Ford versus Nissan, I never would have guessed Ford would win. Wonderful insights into late-twentieth-century American industrial management techniques. When the car guys wanted money to build bigger paint ovens, Ford President Robert McNamara suggested cutting the cars in half before painting them. I guess it also explains a lot about Vietnam.

Gay Hendricks, Ph.D., and Kate Ludeman, Ph.D., *The Corporate Mystic*, Bantam Books, 1996; ISBN 055337494X.

> One of the groups Ron and Ann work with recommends this book to all of their employees. It addresses integrity, leadership, and working with others. Excellent.

James A. Highsmith III, *Adaptive Software Development*, Dorset House, 1999; ISBN 0932633404.

> Jim's book describes how to bring teamwork, speed, and adaptability to larger-scale projects. We'd say that he copied our ideas, except that he got there first. Powerful and deep material in a compact and readable form.

Watts S. Humphrey, *Managing Technical People,* Addison-Wesley, 1997; ISBN 0201545977.

> Good thoughts on group dynamics, innovation, and process. As one might expect from the SEI part of the world, somewhat oppressive, and aimed at larger groups than we address.

Watts S. Humphrey, *The Personal Software Process,* Addison-Wesley, 1997; ISBN 0201548097.

> If you knew all these things about your programming, you'd know something good. You could also win the retention medal for America in the upcoming Olympics. Good ideas, good focus on personal skill. Rather regimented.

Andrew Hunt and David Thomas, *The Pragmatic Programmer*, Addison-Wesley, 2000; ISBN 020161622X.

> A delightful book, demystifying much of programming, bringing it down to earth. "Pragmatic Dave," as we call him to distinguish him from the other important Dave Thomas, has been an active

questioner, indeed inquisitor, and has helped us sharpen our understanding of our ideas. Very XP compatible.

Carole Jackson, *Color Me Beautiful*, Ballantine Books, 1980; ISBN 0345345886.

Why does Jeffries wear so much black? He's a Winter!

Ricky Jay, *Cards as Weapons*, Warner Books, 1988; ISBN 0446387568.

An early precursor to the use of cards for planning and design. Ricky Jay is one of the premier card users of all time.

Bill Jensen, *Simplicity: The New Competitive Advantage in a World of More, Better, Faster*, Perseus Books, 2000; 073820210X.

"Making the complex clear always helps people work smarter. Because it is a lot easier to figure out what's important and ignore what isn't."

Joseph L. Jones and Anita M. Flynn, *Mobile Robots: Inspiration to Implementation*, A K Peters, Ltd., 1998, ISBN 1568810970.

How to build two inexpensive robots, essentially from scratch. Here's a book about a toy you really need!

Brian W. Kernighan and Rob Pike, *The Practice of Programming*, Addison-Wesley, 1999; ISBN 020161586X.

Simplicity, clarity, generality: the cover says it all. Good programmers, especially Extreme ones, profit from having a deep bag of tricks into which they can dig when they need to. Kernighan and Pike show that the tricks need not be complex—the best tricks are delightfully simple.

Brian W. Kernighan and P. J. Plauger, *The Elements of Programming Style*, Second Edition, McGraw-Hill Book Company, 1988; ISBN 0070342075.

The examples aren't in Java (or even C++), but the ideas are still valid.

Donald E. Knuth, *The Art of Computer Programming, Volumes 1–3* Boxed Set, Addison-Wesley, 1998; ISBN 0201485419.

They're expensive, but they're worth it.

Wolfgang Langewiesche, *Stick and Rudder, An Explanation of the Art of Flying*, McGraw-Hill, 1944, 1972; ISBN 0070362408.

> Kent tells a story about learning to drive and how that lesson influenced his ideas on project management. Knowing XP, before learning to fly, has made Chet more aware of their similarities.

Richard A. Lanham, *Revising Business Prose*, Macmillan Publishing Company, 1992; ISBN 0023674806.

> As we revised this book, we tried to follow Lanham's advice. The book is short, simple, and follows its own advice.

Steve Maguire, *Debugging the Development Process: Practical Strategies for Staying Focused, Hitting Ship Dates, and Building Solid Teams*, Microsoft Press, 1994; ISBN 1556155514.

> A thoughtful work on the human side of running a process. I'd not do everything he says here, as I feel the XP processes work better. But the concerns, and many of the practices, are right on.

Steve McConnell, *After the Gold Rush*, Microsoft Press, 1999; ISBN 0735608776.

> McConnell believes that licensing is coming as software development moves into the future. We share a concern over quality and good practice. Our approaches differ substantially, as we lean much more toward simplicity and good internal practices. But read this book.

Steve McConnell, *Code Complete*, Microsoft Press, 1993; ISBN 1556154844.

> Really good material on software construction. Good stuff on personal craftsmanship. Very rubber-meets-road.

Steve McConnell, *Software Project Survival Guide*, Microsoft Press, 1998; ISBN 1572316217.

> We see here the precursors of McConnell's *Gold Rush* thinking. Still, some good advice if rather more draconian than we think necessary. Know thy enemy.

Bertrand Meyer, *Object-Oriented Software Construction*, Second Edition, Prentice Hall, 2000; ISBN 0136291554.

> Quite possibly the best book available on what OO is and what it should be.

Miyamoto Musashi, *A Book of Five Rings*, The Overlook Press, 1974; ISBN 00879510188.

> Originally written in 1645, this book holds the philosophy of Japan's most renowned warrior. He intended this book "for any situation where plans and tactics are used." It's no longer fashionable to kill your programmers with swords, but this is a fascinating book.

Glenford J. Myers, *Reliable Software through Composite Design*, Mason/Charter Publishers, 1975; ISBN 0884052842. Out of print.

> Together with Constantine's work on structured design, one of the seminal works on modularity. High cohesion, low coupling, and just how to build good objects even today.

Sarah O'Keefe, *FrameMaker 5.5.6 for Dummies*, IDG Books, 1999; ISBN 0764506374.

> The one book without which this one could not exist. This, and *Extreme Programming Explained*. The two books . . . oh never mind. Sarah saved our bacon. Thanks, Sarah.

Mark C. Paulk, et al., *The Capability Maturity Model*, Addison-Wesley, 1995; ISBN 0201546647.

> This isn't just "know thy enemy." Yes, CMM can be, has been, and will be misused. However, the goals and the generic activities of CMM are consistent with quality, and worth thinking about. We think you can do without most of the practices, in most situations, but keep them in mind for those sticky situations.

M. Scott Peck, M.D., *The Road Less Travelled*, Simon and Schuster, 1978; ISBN 0671250671.

> There comes a time when we need to take a look at our lives.

Ayn Rand, *The Fountainhead*, Penguin Books, 1943; ISBN 0451191153.

Ayn Rand, *Atlas Shrugged*, Penguin Books, 1957; ISBN 0451191145.

> Individual responsibility and individual mastery are at the core of team performance. It doesn't hurt to start with Rand's vision of the competent man. Just don't stop there.

James Rumbaugh, Michael Blaha, William Premerlani, Frederick Eddy, and William Lorenson, *Object-Oriented Modeling and Design*, Prentice Hall, 1991; ISBN 0136298419.

Elaine St. James, *Simplify Your Life: 100 Ways to Slow Down and Enjoy the Things That Really Matter*, Hyperion, 1994; ISBN 0786880007.

> A small book with lots of advice for thinking about your life and what's really important.

Michael Schrage, *Serious Play*, Harvard Business School Press, 2000; ISBN 0875848141.

> Collaboration, play, "Demo or Die." Learning what you want comes from playing with what might be. Schrage offers prototyping as a way of life. XP suggests making your prototypes real.

Guy L. Steele, Jr., et al., *The Hacker's Dictionary*, Harper & Row, 1983; ISBN 0060910828.

> "BOGOSITY—the degree to which something is bogus. *See* auto-bogophobia, a fear of becoming bogotified."

Philip Toshio Sudo, *Zen Computer*, Simon and Schuster, 1999; ISBN 0684854090.

> This short book asks us to acknowledge the spiritual, meditative side of ourselves as we work with the computers we face every day. It's not deep, not heavy. Rather, it's mild and calming. Good preparation for facing the Blue Screen of Death.

Dave Thomas, *Spicy Chicken Sandwich*, Fresh Every Day, 2000; 213 grams of fat, 410 calories.

> One of the other Daves. Good cook; we don't know about his programming.

Sun Tzu, *The Art of War*, Delta, 1999; ISBN 0385299850.

> Life is a battlefield. Plan to win.

Gerald M. Weinberg, *The Psychology of Computer Programming*, Dorset House Publishing, 1998; ISBN 0932633420.

> This is the silver anniversary edition! Way back in '71, Weinberg made it clear that programming is a people business, not a technical business. Why won't Ron ever learn?

Gerald M. Weinberg, *Quality Software Management, Systems Thinking,* Dorset House, 1992; ISBN 0932633226.

Gerald M. Weinberg, *Quality Software Management, First-Order Measurement,* Dorset House, 1993; ISBN 0932633242.

Gerald M. Weinberg, *Quality Software Management, Volume 3, Congruent Action,* Dorset House, 1994; ISBN 0932633285.

Gerald M. Weinberg, *Quality Software Management, Volume 4, Anticipating Change,* Dorset House, 1997; ISBN 0932633323.

Gerald M. Weinberg, *The Secrets of Consulting,* Dorset House Publishing, 1985, ISBN 0932633013.

> Weinberg brings his usual good humor and good advice together in this book about "the irrational world of consulting." Ron likes to read it in the evenings after a rough day with a client.

Gerald M. Weinberg, *Understanding the Professional Programmer,* Dorset House, 1998; ISBN 0932633099.

> Are you a programmer? Weinberg can help you understand why you are the way you are, and how to be a better one. Hang out with programmers? Read this book in self-defense.

Garry Willis, *Lincoln at Gettysburg, The Words That Remade America,* Touchtone Books, 1993; ISBN 0671867423.

> How those 272 words we memorized in school changed the meaning of the Constitution. A reminder that a powerful message simply expressed can change the world.

Rebecca Wirfs-Brock, Brian Wilkerson, and Lauren Wiener, *Designing Object-Oriented Software,* Prentice Hall, 1990; ISBN 0136298257.

Edward Yourdon, *Death March,* Prentice Hall, 1997; ISBN 0137483104.

> The most depressing book Chet has ever read, and he was an economics major. Yourdon almost seems to approve of the march and tries to help people make the best of it. XP is about avoiding the death march. You might like that better.

Edward Yourdon, *Decline and Fall of the American Programmer*, Prentice Hall, 1994; ISBN 013191958X.

Yourdon predicts the end of the world as we know it.

Edward Yourdon, *Rise and Resurrection of the American Programmer*, Prentice Hall, 1996; ISBN 013121831X.

Yourdon becomes an optimist.

Edward Yourdon and Larry L. Constantine, *Structured Design: Fundamentals of a Discipline of Computer Program and Systems Design*, Prentice Hall, 1986; ISBN 0138544719.

Good material on the use of coupling and cohesion. Applies even now, in these days of objects.

William Zinsser, *On Writing Well*, HarperCollins, 1998; ISBN 0062735233.

We hesitate to list books on writing here. We've tried to follow this good advice. To the extent that we have fallen short, we blame these other books for being unclear or difficult. And, of course, it's Chet's fault anyway.

Index

Stories, *continued*
    tracking and reporting, 137–138
    See also Estimation, Tasks
Stub method, 99
Sum object, 108
SUnit, 105

T
Tasks, 63–64
    estimating, 132–133, 186–187
    releasing, 72
    size, a few days, 153
    See also Stories
Tax package program, 52
"Technical stories," 29
Test-first programming, 70, 72
    Smalltalk example, 107–120
Testing, 234–241
    classes, 99, 101–103, 235
    and code quality, 83–85, 200–201,
        234–235
    database, 99–100
    defects, 163, 166, 169–170, 234
    functional, *see* Acceptance tests
    LDAP problem, 204–210
    methods, 235–236
    tracking and reporting, 138–143
    user interface, 103, 211–223
    See also Acceptance tests; Feedback;
        Unit tests
Thomas, David, 80
Time, 136, 138
    See also Estimating; Tracking
Tracking, 135–145
    defects, 163
    estimates, 152–155, 231
    quality, 138–143
    release level, 158–159
    scope, 136–138
    Tracker, 153, 155

U
Unit tests, 72, 93–103
    and acceptance tests, 102
    classes, 99, 101–103
    databases, 99–100

defects, 163, 166, 169–170
frameworks, *see* jUnit, pyUnit, xUnit
    see also Web site
GUIs, 103, 211–223
real-time/multithreading errors, 103
releasing code, 97, 122–123
speed, 100–101
steps in, 99
tracking and reporting, 138–139
Use case, *see* Stories
User, *see* Customer
User interface, 103, 211–223
User stories. *See* Stories

V
Validation, 243–244
Values, xvi, 172, *see also*
    Aggressiveness (renamed Courage)
    Communication
    Feedback
    Simplicity
    Testing (renamed Feedback)
Variables, *See also* Quality, Resources,
    Scope, Time
VBUnit, 105
Velocity, project, 58–59, 179, 181
'vi', 204–205
Visual Age for Java Professional Edition
    (VAJ), 205

W
Wake, Bill, 211
Web site, www.XProgramming.com
Widgets, 213–214, 220–222
Williams, Laurie, 88
with:with:, 112

X
XP Practices, *see* Practices
XP Values, *see* Values
XP Variables, *see* Variables
xUnit, 105–106